Top shelf.

Wax Poetics and Maker's Mark.

The new album from Brazilian singer SEU JORGE and the band Almaz: PUPILLO, LUCIO MAIA (Nação Zumbi) and ANTONIO PINTO.

Songs famous within the Brazilian diaspora (Tim Maia, Jorge Ben) mesh with classic American (Roy Ayers, Michael Jackson) and European (Kraftwerk, Cane and Able) soul songs begging for a bit of psychedelic samba.

The result?

"Absolutely brilliant..."
- Gilles Peterson, BBC

North America: 07.27.10
Europe: 09.14.10

VP RECORDS PRESENTS
THE SOULFUL SOUNDS OF
BERES HAMMOND

ORIGINAL REMASTERED ALBUM FROM 1979 FEATURING RARE AND UNRELEASED TRACKS!

7" SINGLE AVAILABLE FOR THE FIRST TIME SINCE ITS INITIAL RELEASE OVER 30 YEARS AGO!

2 CD/3 LP COLLECTION OF BERES' GREATEST HITS FROM HIS DAYS WITH ZAP POW THROUGH HIS EXTENSIVE SOLO CAREER

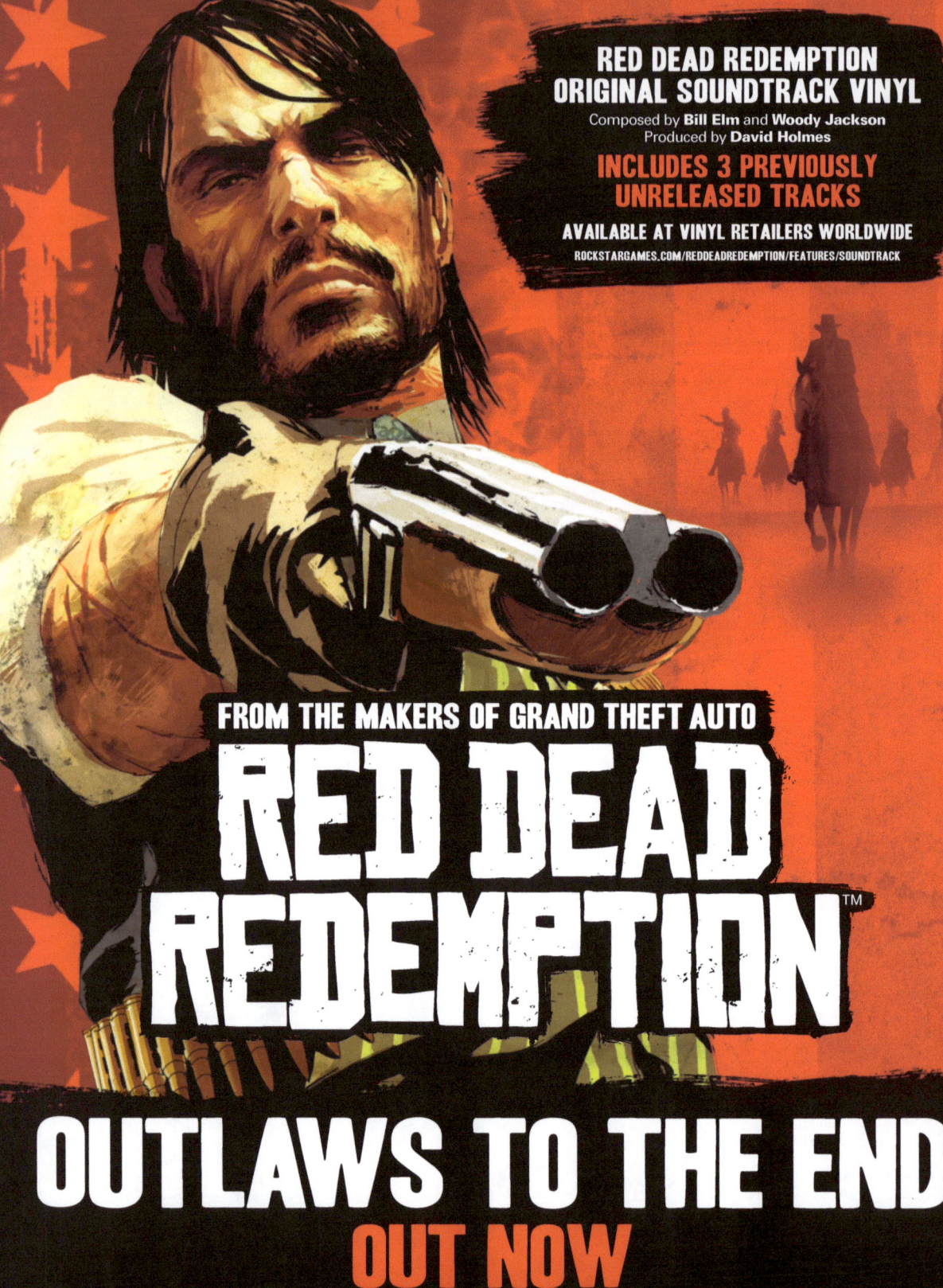

waxpoetics

Editor's Letter	13
Re:Discovery	16
Bilal	26
Spree Wilson	28
The Bamboos	30
Kings Go Forth	32
Record Rundown	36
Studio Rundown	42
Melvin Bliss	46
Erykah Badu	54
Gil Scott-Heron	60
Barry White	70
D'Angelo	82
An Oral History of the Wah-Wah Pedal	92
Ernie Hines	104
Analog Out	112

Front Cover #1
Barry White
Photo by Bobby Holland/Cache Agency

Front Cover #2
Gil Scott-Heron
Photo by Chuck Stewart

Back Cover #1
D'Angelo
Photo by Beth Herzhaft

Back Cover #2
Erykah Badu
Photo by Paige K. Parsons courtesy of Motown/Universal

waxpoetics

WAX POETICS, INC.
45 Main Street,
Suite 516
Brooklyn, NY 11201
p 866.999.4WAX
f 718.624.5695
info@waxpoetics.com
waxpoetics.com

Advertise
advertise@waxpoetics.com
or call 718.624.5696 x203

Subscribe
waxpoetics.com/subscribe
subscribe@waxpoetics.com

Retail
retail@waxpoetics.com
or contact Melanie Raucci,
Disticor Magazine
Distribution Services, at
631.587.1160
mraucci@disticor.com

Contribute
editorial@waxpoetics.com

Editor-in-Chief
Andre Torres

Editor
Brian DiGenti

Marketing Director
Dennis Coxen

Art Directors
Joshua Dunn
Freddy Allen Anzures

Copy Editor
Tom McClure

Editorial Assistant
Brad Farberman

Graphic Designer
Alex Rhea

Contributing Editors
Robbie Busch
Andrew Mason
Ronnie Reese
Matt Rogers

Contributing Writers
Travis Atria
Marisa Aveling
Angus Batey
Robbie Busch
Brad Farberman
Michael A. Gonzales
Gerald Jensen
Jonathan Kirby
Peter Kirn
Daniel Margolis
Ronnie Reese
Patrick Sisson
Alex Suskind
Allen Thayer
Dave Tompkins
Charles Waring

Contributing Photographers
Eric Coleman
Kenneth Cappello
Nikita Gale
Bode Helm
Beth Herzhaft
Bobby Holland
Laurens Van Houten
Josh Jensen
Jim Newberry
Paige K. Parsons
Matt Rogers
Chuck Stewart

Sales Manager
Michael Coxen
Account Executives
Amir Abdullah
Paul Alexander
Damian Ashton
Sharan Singh
Customer Service Manager
Ben Arsenault
Record Label Manager
Amir Abdullah
Special Projects
Bertram Jay Haine
Linh Truong
Accounts Receivable
Connie S. Reale

Interns
Mohamed Bourgiuba
Stephanie Chu
Guin Frehling
Alex Govenar
Olivia Klugh
Paulina Mandeville
Brian Renda
Stephen Sajkowsky
Steve So

Published by **Wax Poetics, Inc.**
Printed by **MGM Printing Group**
Distributed by **Disticor Magazine Distribution Services**

© 2010 Wax Poetics, Inc.
All rights reserved. Unauthorized duplication without prior consent is prohibited.
ISSN 1537-8241

NICK ROSEN
INTO THE SKY

A CREATION OF
RARE BEAUTY
BY MEMBERS OF
BUILD AN ARK
PRODUCED & INCLUDING ARRANGEMENTS BY
MIGUEL ATWOOD-FERGUSON
(FLYING LOTUS, SUITE FOR MA DUKES)
AND VOCAL CONTRIBUTIONS BY
MIA DOI TODD

**AVAILABLE JULY 20TH
CD / LP+7" / DIGITAL**

LP INCLUDES DIGITAL DOWNLOAD
PLUS 7" WITH B-SIDE REMIX BY
**CARLOS NIÑO &
JESSE PETERSON**
(AVAILABLE EXCLUSIVELY THROUGH LP)

ALBUM RELEASE PARTY CO-SPONSORED BY waxpoetics & dublab

LA: JULY 30 / 8 PM @ THE LATC (LOS ANGELES THEATRE CENTER)
WITH DJ SETS BY CARLOS NIÑO AND FROSTY
NYC: AUG 5 / 8 PM @ THE LOCAL 269

IN-STORE PERFORMACES AT: POO-BAH RECORDS (LA) JULY 27 / 7PM
DOWNTOWN MUSIC GALLERY (NYC) AUG 1 / 6PM

WWW.PORTERRECORDS.COM

waxpoetics

On the heels of our third Hip-Hop Issue comes our first to look solely at rhythm and blues. Technically, just about everything we get into here is rhythm and blues, or R&B as most people know it. While we favor the old-school classic type, R&B means a lot of different things to a lot of different people. To some, it's Bo Diddley; to others, it's Trey Songz. My relationship with R&B was typical for any hip-hop kid trying to keep it real in the late '80s/early '90s. You just didn't mess with it. Though hip-hop started out with MCs rhyming over popular R&B tracks of the day, it eventually found its voice beyond those already worn grooves. But once R&B started jacking hip-hop beats, it became "Rap and Bullshit" to most heads who were trying to keep it more "rough, rugged, and raw" than on a "smoothed-out tip." There have been a few notable exceptions over the years, but truthfully, most of what we're hearing being paraded as R&B today is barely distinguishable from the so-called hip-hop we hear. It's almost as if the two forms fused into a more conveniently labeled "urban" muzak that somehow lacks the best of both sources. Looking at the state of R&B today, I realize that I could say the same about R&B that I said about hip-hop in the last issue. Most of the music is lackluster at best and the quality so low that much of it hardly qualifies as R&B, being devoid of both *rhythm* and *blues*.

Like last issue, we hope this joint will serve as inspiration to the young and old alike who are in pursuit of freeing minds and asses the world over. Again, it's another double cover with a few heavyweights who have changed the game. Barry White b/w D'Angelo and Gil Scott-Heron b/w Erykah Badu is a lineup that tells a story unto itself. It's not the obvious setup, and that's exactly why we're rocking with it. This is our rhythm and blues. The R&B that we will lay claim to. So if we're going here, the king of baby-making music, Barry White, has to be at the center. A troubadour in the classic sense, Barry's undeniable bass baritone and orchestral flair became the blueprint for seduction and set the stage for an entire generation of wannabe Casanovas. From the dance floor to the bedroom, Barry's insistent grooves and conversational approach on the mic have become staples for any cat trying to spit game. But Gil Scott-Heron spits another kind of game. This is the true master to whom there is no father to his style. A poet working in the troubadour tradition, Gil wasn't purely concerned with love in the romantic sense. He took R&B and flipped it with a sword-like tongue, delivering incisive thoughts on the world and the human condition at large. Gil laid the foundation for the future of Black youth to fully understand freedom of expression. Two artists from that generation came up in the post-hip-hop-meets-R&B world but were able to express true artistry with this new sound. D'Angelo and Erykah Badu were both so unique, they were set up as the king and queen of the ill-fated "neo-soul" movement. But the unfortunate title couldn't hold back the music's organic approach—merging R&B and hip-hop in a way that attempted to bring out the best of both sides. They are from a very small group of artists who can singlehandedly restore one's faith in R&B. This is not a group of mere performers and entertainers; these are artists whose impact is still being felt today.

Over the years I've come to understand the full scope of rhythm and blues, and in the end have realized it's at the core of everything I love. It's the foundation of modern music as I know it. It's jazz, it's rock and roll, it's soul, it's funk, it's disco, it's hip-hop. It's that thing that keeps asses shaking and, since its inception, has manifested itself in a myriad of ways over many decades. It's the deep well we go to fill up on, the real chicken soup for the soul. Or better yet, fried chicken for the soul. So we're back serving as a guidepost and calling for a realignment of the music. We never play it safe and continue to push the boundaries of knowledge and myopic categorizations. We just hope the music can do the same.

Slow-jammed,

Andre Torres

(RIP Rammellzee)

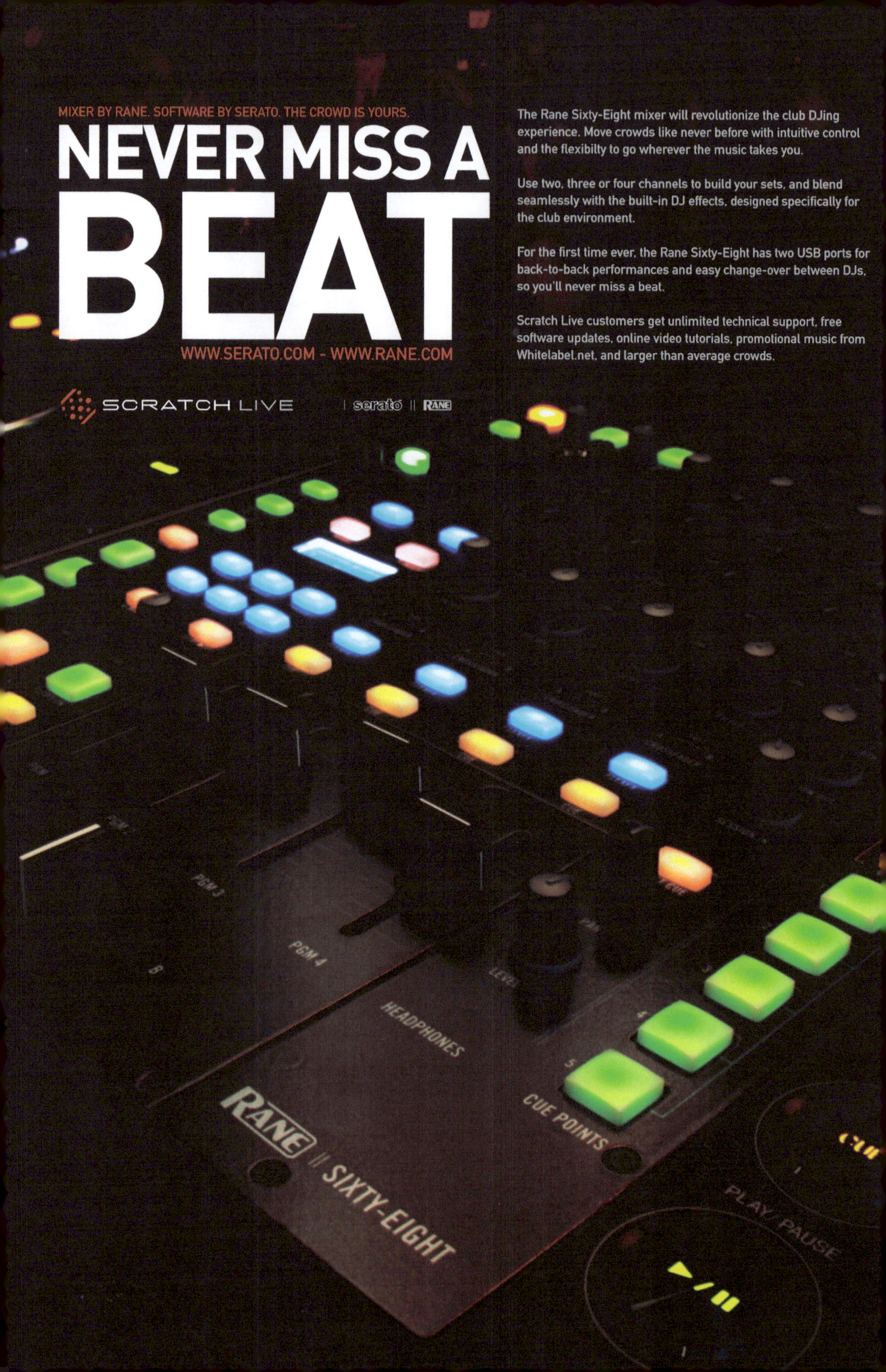

MIXER BY RANE. SOFTWARE BY SERATO. THE CROWD IS YOURS.
NEVER MISS A BEAT
WWW.SERATO.COM - WWW.RANE.COM
The Rane Sixty-Eight mixer will revolutionize the club DJing experience. Move crowds like never before with intuitive control and the flexibilty to go wherever the music takes you.
Use two, three or four channels to build your sets, and blend seamlessly with the built-in DJ effects, designed specifically for the club environment.
For the first time ever, the Rane Sixty-Eight has two USB ports for back-to-back performances and easy change-over between DJs, so you'll never miss a beat.
Scratch Live customers get unlimited technical support, free software updates, online video tutorials, promotional music from Whitelabel.net, and larger than average crowds.
SCRATCH LIVE
serato
RANE
PGM 3
PGM 4
HEADPHONES
CUE POINTS
RANE
SIXTY-EIGHT
PLAY / PAUSE

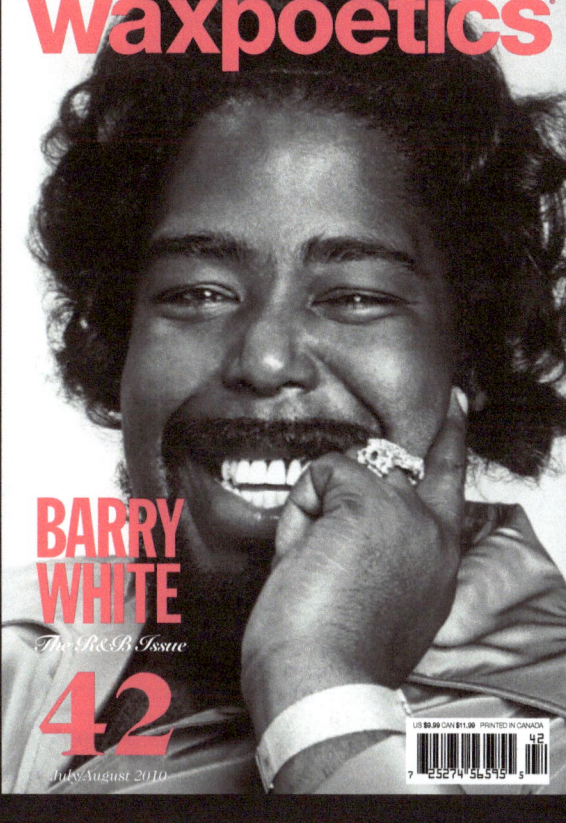

waxpoetics

BARRY WHITE
The R&B Issue
42
July/August 2010

LISTEN TO THIS ISSUE

Download any **Wax Poetics Issue Playlist** and be automatically entered for a chance to win a **Rane Serato Scratch LIVE**

Visit **digital.waxpoetics.com/playlist** for our ten-track mix of this issue.

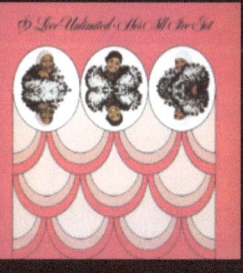
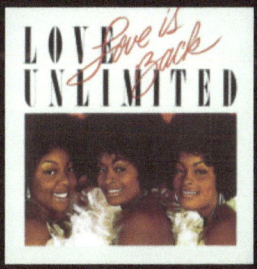

waxpoetics

Tito Ramos
Where My Head Is At
(Cotique) 1972

It was 1972. The ghetto was in full bloom and after a deep breath, our man Tito "Big T" Ramos was getting ready to put in his bid for change. Big T had been riding high on the Meditation. He had battled with the *Boogaloo Blues*, before taking a short trip with *Subway Joe*. But the '60s were behind him, and El Barrio was bathing in the afterglow while bracing for a new day. Tito was coming off a highly productive period in his musical life, but, as he says, "We were kind of crazy, messing around with LSD and partying day and night." Big T saw himself reflected in a world that was consuming its own tail. A year earlier, Marvin Gaye had asked *What's Going On*? Now, there was something swelling in Harlem—Spanish or otherwise. T's head was still fuzzy after burning too long in the heat of the TnT explosion. Big T, while not mild-mannered, was a gentle soul who had been tossed around by the music industry for the better part of a decade. His side-kick through most of his adventures had been Tony Rojas, the other half of the salsa/boogaloo outfit the TnT Band. But he knew his last outing was to be a solo mission.

Needing a break, he stared himself down and said, "I need to see what direction I actually want to go in." He spent six months in his house. "Every day, I was just writing the songs and living them. [This record] was really a part of me." Spiritually, Tito was on a love kick, while musically, he drew on everything from his early days singing on street corners in Spanish Harlem to contemporary "modern soul" and freaked-out acid funk. "Motown was big at the time, so there was a lot of influence," he remembers. "There was a lot of doo-wop mixed with Motown. See, I always say that the type of music that I do is Latin-soul-jazz. It's a fusion, because we used a lot of jazz riffs with the horns, and then we [put in] the R&B with the Latin rhythm."

The drugs and haze that had been constant companions had opened him up to a new world. But now Big T saw the bigger picture. He was about to hip you to a little something. And tell you where his head was at. As he looked out over El Barrio with pride, he preached that most basic and beautiful idea: "Love is something that we all need." ● **Robbie Busch**

JAZZMAN PRESENTS...
THE HOLY GRAIL SERIES

ROY BROOKS & THE ARTISTIC TRUTH
ETHNIC EXPRESSIONS JMANCD/LP 034

Staggeringly rare live spiritual jazz set, originally released in tiny quantities in 1973, on the independent Im-Hotep label.

BOBBY JACKSON
THE CAFE EXTRA-ORDINAIRE STORY JMANCD/LP 035

Superb spiritual, modal and progressive jazz recording, documenting Jackson and his Minneapolis live venue in 1970.

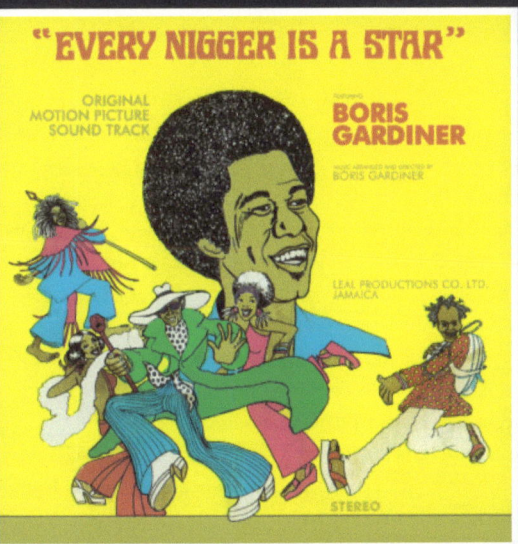

THE BORIS GARDINER HAPPENING
EVERY NIGGER IS A STAR JMANCD/LP 036

Perhaps the rarest blaxploitation soundtrack in existence, featuring solid ghetto funk and roots reggae all the way.

MARVIN PETERSON & THE SOULMASTERS
IN CONCERT JMANCD/LP 037

Ultra-rare 'Dimension 70' release featuring a heavyweight live session, showcasing Peterson's first foray into soul and funk.

A SERIES DEDICATED TO BRINGING YOU ONLY **THE RAREST OF THE RARE**, WITH LIMITED NUMBERED VINYL AND DELUXE COMPACT DISC EDITIONS FEATURING REMASTERED SOUND, ARTIST BIOGRAPHIES AND UN-SEEN ARCHIVE PHOTOS

WORLDWIDE MAIL ORDER FROM: WWW.JAZZMANRECORDS.CO.UK

re:Discovery

Curtis Mayfield
There's No Place Like America Today
(Curtom Records) 1975

Think things are bad now? America was going through *them changes* in 1975. On January 1 of that year, four of Nixon's top men were convicted of conspiracy, obstruction of justice, and perjury for their involvement in the Watergate scandal. In September, President Ford was nearly assassinated *twice*. A heavy recession had taken hold. And unemployment reached nearly nine percent.

Lucky for us, Curtis Mayfield was there to turn it all into music. From the deep clavinet riffs of "Billy Jack" to the hopeful horn lines of "Love to the People," 1975's *There's No Place Like America Today* is the restless, searching sound of a country coming undone—but refusing to give up. Slow and pensive, the funk of *America* is miles away from the exuberant sounds of *Curtis* or *Super Fly*. No one was serious, and it made Mayfield furious.

And you could feel it in the album art. Illustrated by Peter Palombi, *America*'s cover features a dapper-looking White man behind the wheel of a car filled with pretty women. Juxtaposed is an all-Black breadline. It's a fitting accompaniment to the music on *America*, especially the anthemic Curtis original "Hard Times," not to be confused with David "Fathead" Newman's trademark track of the same name.

Famously recorded by Baby Huey in 1970—and by Gene Chandler as "In My Body's House" before that—Curtis finally tackled this one himself in '75. Dark and foreboding, and marked by mournful wah-wah guitar and Quinton Joseph's stellar, just-the-facts drumming, "Hard Times" finds Curtis confronting the reality of Black-on-Black crime: "From my body house, I see, like me, another / Familiar face of creed and race, a brother / But to my surprise, I found another man corrupt / Although he be my brother, he wants to hold me up."

But the real sparks fly on the aforementioned "Billy Jack," a companion piece to the far-more-visible "Freddie's Dead." To begin, keyboardist Rich Tufo spells out a chilly bass line in three-note fragments. Henry Gibson's congas and a chunky rhythm guitar part emerge from the ether. Thirty seconds in, we hear a snare crack, and a quiet, menacing groove has arrived. Like Freddie, Billy is a tragic character, dead before the song's begun. But Curtis lacks the sympathy he felt in 1972. "It's a wonder he lived this long," sings Curtis.

Thirty-five years after the release of *America*, the unemployment rate in the U.S. is at a whopping 9.7 percent, and we're once again in the throes of a punishing recession. I guess there's no place like America *any day*. And I guess we still need this music to pull us through. ● **Brad Farberman**

101
WWW.101APPAREL.COM

TONY ALLEN "AFRO BEAT-SINCE 1969"
TONY ALLEN T-SHIRT W/ DJ MIX CONTAINING TONY ALLEN UNRELEASED REMIXES, B-SIDES AND CLASSICS MIXED BY DJ RICH MEDINA.

Tony Allen has long been acknowledged as Africa's finest kit drummer and one of the continent's most influential musicians. His playing draws on four different styles – highlife, soul/funk, jazz and traditional Nigerian drumming. A unique and mighty sound. Together with Fela Kuti Allen co-created Afrobeat. its an honor to present this exclusive t-shirt & mix cd.

View the full collection of Men's and Women's apparel and accessories along with our exclusive artist mix cd & t-shirt collaborations with Tony Allen, Dam-Funk, Quantic, Kon & Amir, Nightmares on Wax and more at:

ww.101apparel.com

TONY ALLEN T-SHIRT GRAPHIC

WWW.NONESUCH.COM

PHOTOS BY : RAYMOND J. DUMAS

re:Discovery

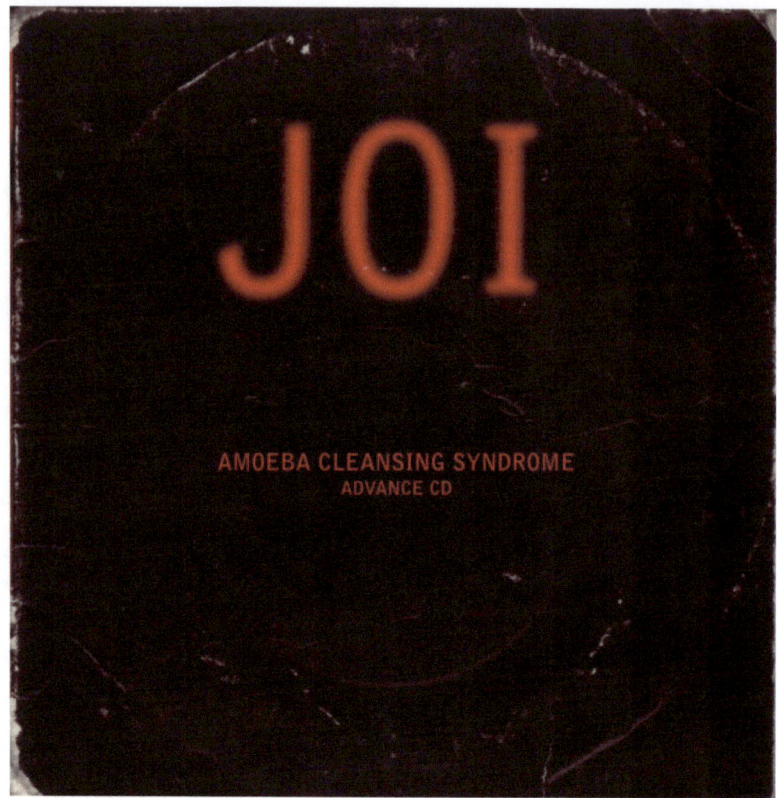

Joi
Amoeba Cleansing Syndrome
(Freeworld Recordings) 1997

In the 1990s, Atlanta was a hothouse of post-new-jack-swing R&B. Yet, while most producers were content making safe Black pop for the masses, Dallas Austin wanted to be an auteur. While he'd constructed platinum-selling singles for ABC, TLC, and Boyz II Men, the wicked keyboardist had grown up admiring the artistry of Prince's cyberfunk manifesto, *1999*, and wanted to make a difference.

"You've got to do what people want you to do before you can do what you want to do," Austin said in 1992. Two years later, he introduced the world to glam singer Joi. A lipstick liberator in the age of prefab divas, her 1994 debut, *The Pendulum Vibe*, was a wonderful introduction to an arty funk-rock aesthetic.

Still, it was Joi's sophomore joint, *Amoeba Cleansing Syndrome*, that was supposed to set the world on fire. "My vision was simple," she explained in 1997. "I want to do funky, groundbreaking stuff."

Although Joi, who has sung with OutKast and Curtis Mayfield, had no problem referring to herself as R&B, her style was as influenced by the sci-fi imagery of *Barbarella* and P-Funk as she was by the midnight wail of Gladys Knight.

Recruiting wild boys Fishbone to serve as her backing band, Joi returned to the studio with Austin (more coconspirator than Svengali), Organized Noize, Whild Peach, and boyfriend Big Gipp, who contributed country-ass ad libs to the upbeat radio single "Ghetto Superstar."

"We are here to take you on an aural expectation," Joi says on the introduction, "Welcome Amoeba Spirit," before kick-starting the disc with the booming "Move On," which combines gutbucket soul, rock guitars, and Paradise Garage grooves. Later, Joi shows her true colors by segueing into a mighty cover of Betty Davis's "If I'm Lucky (I Might Just Get Picked Up)."

"I heard George Clinton talking about Davis's work, but it was actually Fishbone member JB who played me her songs," Joi said. In addition, she covered Labelle's raunchy "You Turn Me On," a song from their acclaimed *Nightbirds*. "Labelle was like superheroes to me."

Writing lyrics for all original material, Joi could be so revealing, she sounded naked. On the bluesy "Hurts Sometimes" and the orgasmic "Dirty Mind," she flaunts her freak flag without shame. Yet, when teaming with sonic architects Organized Noize on the psychedelic "Dandelion Dust," she sounds fragile as Liz Fraser from the Cocteau Twins.

Too cutting edge for Joi's original label, EMI, *Amoeba Cleansing Syndrome* was rejected in 1997. Dallas Austin bought the album back for his Freeworld imprint and scheduled a January 1998 release, but the label soon folded. Fortunately, hundreds of advance copies were distributed to reviewers, journalists, and radio; bootlegs are easily obtained. ○ **Michael A. Gonzales**

NEW RELEASES DISTRIBUTED BY FORCED EXPOSURE

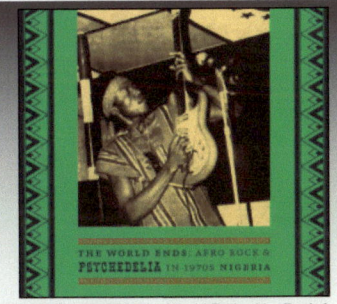

VARIOUS ARTISTS *The World Ends: Afro Rock & Psychedelia in 1970s Nigeria* 2CD/3LP

Soundway presents 32 forgotten nuggets that represent the heavy, gritty and sometimes edgy side of Nigeria's most musically prolific decade. Spread over 2 CDs and 2 triple gatefold LPs, the fuzzed-out, electrifying grooves featured here are the sound of a generation of young musicians fusing hard-rock and psychedelia with funk and traditional rhythms.

KENNY GRAHAM AND HIS SATELLITES *Moondog And Suncat Suites* CD/LP

Trunk presents a first-time ever reissue of this very rare 1957 album of British jazz interpretations of **Moondog** originals, with an exceptional line-up featuring **Stan Tracey, Phil Seamen, Danny Moss** and **Ivor Slaney**, engineered by **Joe Meek**. With soaring vocalists and a host of strange instruments, the Viking of Sixth Avenue never sounded so exotic, ethereal and timeless.

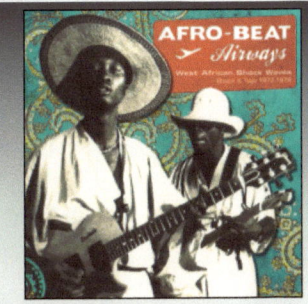

VARIOUS ARTISTS *Afro-Beat Airways: West African Shock Waves – Ghana & Togo 1972-1979* CD/2LP

Organ-driven Afro-beat, cosmic funk and raw, psychedelic boogie are just some of the flavors to be found on this highly danceable compilation by **Samy Ben Redjeb**, founder of Analog Africa. *Afro-Beat Airways* showcases an amazing diversity of vintage West African sounds and includes a gorgeous 44-page, full-color booklet with rare pictures and extensive liner notes.

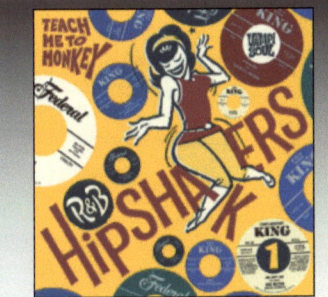

VARIOUS ARTISTS *R&B Hipshakers Vol. 1: Teach Me To Monkey* CD/10x7" BOX

WFMU's "Downtown Soulville" DJ **Mr. Fine Wine** dips into the Federal and King label vaults to present this uptempo and danceable collection of '60s R&B and early soul. Crazy dances, intense guitar instrumentals and mind-altering sides from the likes of **Eddie Kirk, The Drivers, The "5" Royales** and more.

VARIOUS ARTISTS *Cumbia Beat Volume 1: Experimental Guitar-Driven Tropical Sounds from Peru 1966-1976* 2CD/2LP

The first volume in Vampisoul's new series dedicated to Peruvian cumbia. Tropical genres such as merengue, guaracha, rumba and cumbia mix with '60s beat and psychedelic rock, while electric guitars reinterpret folk melodies and traditions from the Andes and the Amazonian jungle.

ANIBAL VELASQUEZ Y SU CONJUNTO *Mambo Loco* CD/LP

Legendary accordionist **Anibal Velasquez** has been one of the most prolific musicians of Colombia's Musica Tropical movement. Analog Africa pays tribute to one of the few living legends of the country's glorious musical past with a collection of his sensational music, a heady blend of guaracha, cumbia and infectious African beats. *"It will rock a party."* –The New York Times

VARIOUS ARTISTS *I'm Going Where The Water Drinks Like Wine — 18 Unsung Bluesmen: Rarities 1923-1929* CD/LP

The latest volume in Sub Rosa's "Fundamental" series is devoted to rare and lost blues rarities from virtual unknowns circa the 1920s. Utterly compulsive listening from start to finish, this collection tells an entirely alternative history of the blues, featuring **Bo Weavil Jackson, Willie Baker, Rube Lacey** and more.

VARIOUS ARTISTS *Bustin' Out 1982 - New Wave To New Beat Volume 2* CD

DJ **Mike Maguire** (Juno Reactor) charts the groundbreaking developments in electronic-based music through the '80s. Hugely-influential proto-industrial, dub-funk, and electro classics from **Gary Numan, Front 242, ESG, Afrika Bambaataa, Chris & Cosey, Mark Stewart, Dub Syndicate** and more. Includes in-depth sleeve notes documenting each track.

SOUND IRATION *Sound Iration In Dub* 2CD

Sound Iration's 1989 debut spear-headed a new age in homegrown British reggae, pioneering '80s digi-dub with a sound that's still sought-after by today's dubstep producers. Year Zero's deluxe digipack reissue of this long-fêted milestone includes a fold-out poster booklet and a bonus disc of rare demos, one-off dub plates and unreleased mixes.

these titles available at fine independent record stores and online at www.forcedexposure.com
Retailers: request wholesale information from fe@forcedexposure.com

Jeff Redd
"Show You"
(EMI) 1993

Cookout classics like "I Found Lovin'" and "You Called and Told Me" earned Jeff Redd considerable brass under the new-jack-swing regime. But when the time came to record a follow-up to 1990's hit-laden *A Quiet Storm*, Redd envisioned a body of music more Marvin than "Motownphilly." He enlisted keyboardist/producer Dinky Bingham, who, using natural and artificial flavors, followed Redd's melodic cues to craft the playfully awkward, yet structurally sound, "Show You." Vocally, Redd's tender confessionals were delivered with supreme control, the inventive cadence complementing the unpredictable nature of the instrumental. Drum patterns and coloring courtesy of Lord Finesse would help the track gel, breaking common ground between ballad and banger. "I actually even rapped on it," declares Finesse. "I don't got that version," he laments, "but the rhymes was *nasty*."

"We didn't say, 'These are hits,'" confesses Redd of the writing process. "We just said, 'They *hot*.'" A refreshing disinterest in industry, even audience acceptance, was a unifying ethos among the participants. Finesse maintains, "We didn't think about, 'Oh, let's get played on the radio,' or 'Will this cross over?' That's what makes that music special, because we went with what we felt—and we *felt* it."

Not too hard, not too soft, it seemed that Jeff Redd's tentatively titled *On the Down Low* would lay the cornerstone for a new movement—one where young-folks music and grown-folks music collided. But when EMI shuttered their Black music department, *Down Low* was left without a home.

"I'm going to blame it on the record companies," says Bingham of the team's thwarted efforts. "Jeff Redd basically would have created neo-soul had his album blown up. The record companies were scared to take a chance. But as soon as D'Angelo came out? He had an A&R who cared; he had an A&R who said, 'I'm taking the chance.'"

Although Redd transitioned to a successful A&R position at MCA, he's remembered best as a performer, a career he has recently resumed. "You know, when you don't have big sales," he says, "you think that it was just a flop. Then you find out years later that people wanted that record, that people wanted you to come overseas. That's what we're working on now. I want to do Japan, I want to do London, Amsterdam—I want to do all those places. And I'm going to." ● Jon Kirby

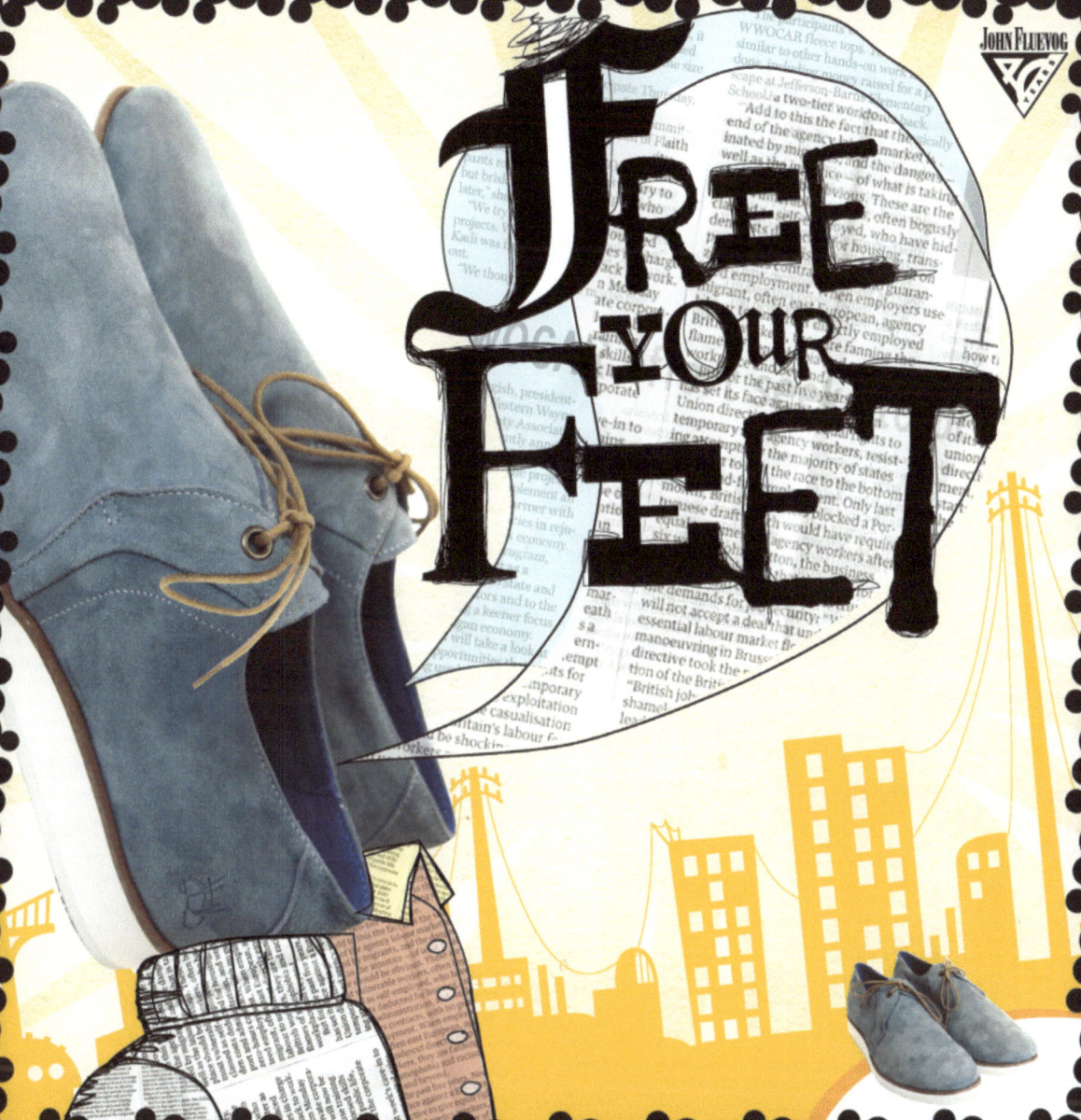

re:Discovery

D.J. Rogers
D.J. Rogers
(Shelter Records) 1973

"Because I write songs with a message," D.J. Rogers explains at the start of "You Are My Joy" from his 1979 LP, *Trust Me*, "I've been called a philosopher, a messenger, and even a reverend. But I'd like to take time to set the record straight, and let you know I just try to write songs that get people from Monday to Tuesday. I believe if you sing about the problem, you're obligated to sing about the answer."

Writers are advised to eschew the use of clichés, but statements such as this one are why rediscovering just one D.J. Rogers album is akin to choosing one's favorite child. Rogers was an extraordinary talent and a beacon of gospel soul. Spirituality permeates nearly all of his recorded work, and the sermons conveyed through spoken words and lyrics, coupled with a dynamic vocal range and searing tenor, places him in the stratum of pioneers like Donny Hathaway and Rance Allen.

The *D.J. Rogers* debut for Leon Russell and Denny Cordell's Shelter Records label is a self-assured and soul-searching declaration of salvation straight from the pulpit. All songs are written and arranged by Rogers, who had worked under the direction of Harrison Johnson in the Los Angeles Community Choir and with the venerable Reverend James Cleveland as director of the Watts Community Choir. The joyful opening track "Listen to the Message" sets a prophetic tone. "Where There's a Will" follows, with the phrase "I'm not what I want to be, but I'm not what I used to be" that would be repeated on *Trust Me* as proof of a message remaining consistent over the course of a career. Maxayn and a pre-Mandre Andre Lewis provide backing vocals and bass guitar respectively, with Rogers directing full choir vocals from the Stanley Lee Ensemble on "Watch Out for the Riders," "Celebration," and what is arguably the album's centerpiece: a gorgeous, metaphorical eight-minute ode to the hereafter titled "Don't You Want to Ride."

For the remainder of the '70s, Rogers would collaborate with the Gap Band, Patrice Rushen, and Deniece Williams, record stellar singles like "Love Brought Me Back," "No Need to Say Goodbye," and "All My Love," and release *Trust Me* and 1978's *Love Brought Me Back* for Maurice White's Kalimba Productions. Unlike many R&B artists with roots in the church, he never separated church and art, and always sought to inspire.

"Singers, keep on singing," Rogers wrote in the liner notes for *Trust Me*. "Musicians, keep on playing; producers, keep on producing; arrangers, keep on arranging.

"The race is not given to the swift nor to the strong, but to the one who endureth to the end." ○ **Ronnie Reese**

ALOE BLACC GOOD THINGS
MADLIB MEDICINE SHOW
TONY COOK BACK TO REALITY
MAYER HAWTHORNE STRANGE ARRANGEMENT
DAM-FUNK TOEACHIZOWN
WWW.STONESTHROW.COM

Photo by Eric Coleman for www.mochilla.com

Bilal
Philly soul cat comes full circle

Let it be known: this time around, Bilal is not about love songs. "The way I've been writing on this album, I've really just been writing for me. Does that sound selfish?" he asks with a laugh. "I'm just not in that place. A lot of the songs are self-searching tunes and political tunes, but that's where I'm at right now."

Guest spots aside, it's been a good few years since we've received official word from the Philadelphia native. If you don't count the leaked, yet widely lauded, *Love for Sale* album back in 2006, the last full-length studio release we saw from Bilal was his 2001 debut, *1st Born Second*. In this silence, however, the vocalist worked through his own demons, both professional and personal, culminating in the release of *Airtight's Revenge*.

The story of Bilal's third album starts where the leak left him four years ago. Already feeling compromised by a major label and its constant demand for hits, the bootlegging of what was to be Bilal's second LP simply added force to the blow. He found himself grinding to a standstill, and experiencing writer's block. "I went through a phase where I just hated doing [music]," Bilal explains. "I hated the process of making it, because I felt like I was just making a bunch of contrived stuff. So I stopped for a minute."

To extract himself from that clouded head space, Bilal took to the road, playing shows that arose in response to *Love for Sale*. To his surprise, people would approach him after the show, expressing how much they liked the material that Interscope had all but discarded. This positive feedback from audiences helped Bilal rebuild his confidence. While his immediate intention was to shift away from making music, a lack of pressure spurred him to secretly create again, to write and put together songs in hotel rooms using Apple's GarageBand.

With the help of friend, producer, and drummer in his band, Steve McKie, Bilal started piecing together *Airtight's Revenge* around two years ago. What has finally surfaced is a reflection of an artist working through a number of ways to reprogram and find himself again, with the backing of McKie and the producers Nottz, Shafiq Husayn, and 88-Keys. Like Bilal said, there aren't that many love songs on this release, but it doesn't mean that the content isn't personal.

"I even have a daddy song on this album, 'cause that's the whole thing I go through: being a father and a family man now," Bilal says. "I also have a son who has autism, so that's a whole new level of understanding too. And my youngest son is into music, and he has sickle cell [disease]. So there's a bunch of levels of things that I deal with and that music really helps me understand."

Through the process of soul-searching and rebuilding himself through creation, *Airtight's Revenge* sees Bilal coming full circle. But the search isn't over yet. "You know what's funny about that? The more you search," he ponders before bursting out with a laugh, "you realize, 'Man, why'd I open up this book?' But this is a cool journey. Every day is a lesson."
○ **Marisa Aveling**

THE BUDOS BAND

New Album Available August 10th

LP / CD / DIG

WWW.THEBUDOSBAND.COM
WWW.DAPTONERECORDS.COM

07/13	ANN ARBOR, MI - BLIND PIG
07/15	QUEBEC CITY, QC - INTERNATIONAL SUMMER FESTIVAL
07/16	OTTAWA, ON - CISCO OTTAWA BLUESFEST
07/17	TORONTO, ON - LEE'S PALACE
07/21	PHILADELPHIA, PA - JOHNNY BRENDA'S
07/22	HARRISBURG, PA - THE ABBEY BAR AT ABC
07/23	FLOYD, VA - FLOYDFEST
07/24	WASHINGTON, DC - BLACK CAT
08/07	BROOKLYN, NY - CELEBRATE BROOKLYN!
08/11	SAN DIEGO, CA - THE CASBAH
08/12	LOS ANGELES, CA - LEVITT PAVILION
08/13	PASADENA, CA - LEVITT PAVILION
08/14	SAN LUIS OBISPO, CA - DOWNTOWN BREW
08/15	SAN FRANCISCO, CA - OUTSIDE LANDS @ GOLDEN GATE PARK
08/17	TEMPE, AZ - SAIL INN
08/21	AUSTIN, TX - THE MOHAWK
08/22	DALLAS, TX - GRANADA
08/24	OKLAHOMA CITY, OK - CONSERVATORY
08/25	KANSAS CITY, MO - RECORD BAR
08/27	DENVER, CO - LARIMER LOUNGE
08/28	BOULDER, CO - FOX THEATER
08/29	DURANGO, CO - ABBEY THEATRE
08/31	SALT LAKE CITY, UT - STATE ROOM
09/01	BOISE, ID - THE GROVE PLAZA
09/02	EUGENE, OR - W.O.W. HALL
09/03	PORTLAND, OR - DANTE'S
09/04	SEATTLE, WA - BUMBERSHOOT
10/30	HONOLULU, HI - HALLOWBALOO MUSIC & ARTS FEST

UPCOMING FALL RELEASES INCLUDE A SLEW OF 45'S BY THE BUDOS BAND, BOB & GENE, EL REGO AND MORE AS WELL AS THE DEBUT FULL-LENGTH BY CHARLES BRADLEY & THE MENAHAN STREET BAND, STAY TUNED!

Photo by Nikita Gale

Spree Wilson
Singer-songwriter finds his niche

The mere mention of 1960s counterculture has gotten Spree Wilson riled up—so much so that the twenty-six-year-old MC, guitarist, and producer is now reeling off Dylan lyrics as if they had been hiding under his tongue, waiting to escape: "Once upon a time, you dressed so fine, you threw the bums a dime in your prime, didn't you?"

Raised in Nashville, Tennessee, Spree—born Joseph Young III—was instilled with the spirit of music at an early age. His father sang in a doo-wop band; his mother, grandmother, and great-grandmother all played piano; and his godfather was Billy Cox, the bass player from Band of Gypsys. They would all factor in exposing the culture of music to Spree, who began playing saxophone at age six. Years later, he would teach himself guitar.

"I always realized I could get attention [from people] if I performed in front of them," Spree says with a laugh. "I was a single child, so I craved and yearned for attention. Anytime I had friends over, I would be telling jokes or dancing in the middle of the floor."

But now, Spree isn't just performing; he is on the cusp of trending a new era in hip-hop: the Andre 3000-esque model of combining rapper, songwriter, and musician into one act. His unique blend of poignant lyrics, clever hooks, and a signature croon has already won him support from music heavyweights like Q-Tip and Mark Ronson.

It's all pretty impressive considering that just last June, Spree was homeless in New York City. He moved from Atlanta, where he had been interning at Dallas Austin's studio while working on his own music.

"I had literally played every venue in Atlanta twice…I had been written up in every local paper…and I still [kept] feeling like I was hitting the ceiling," Spree says. "I was like, 'Fuck it.' I woke up one morning and was like, 'I got to get the hell up out of here.' So I sold my car [and] bought a one-way train ticket [to New York]."

After holing up in the New York train station for a week or so, he moved in with a college friend. A few weeks later, he was on the phone with Q-Tip—the legendary rapper was a fan of Spree's music. Now, the Tribe MC is executive producing Spree's debut album, *Plastic Dreams*, due out later this year.

Spree's eclectic songwriting stems from a fascination with hip-hop, classic rock, and 1960s Beat Generation ideals. Spree has been known to evoke names like Jack Kerouac or Allen Ginsberg in his rhymes, and he often uses chord progressions and guitar riffs with '60s flair.

His interest in classic rock began when he was young; the first song he learned on saxophone was the Beatles' "Yellow Submarine." But Spree had a musical revelation after transferring to an arts school at age twelve. "For the first time in my life, I was the minority in my school," says Spree. "[But] these kids would listen to everything…the Beach Boys, the Animals, Bowie. I was so intrigued listening to [rock]."

With a well-received EP (*Evil Angel*) under his belt, Spree hopes to deliver on his first record—a final product that both his musical influences and a general audience can be proud of. "It's kind of like I am starting back from scratch, because I want something that can be on the same level as my heroes," explains Spree. "Just something they could appreciate and something that people on a mass scale can appreciate."

○ Alex Suskind

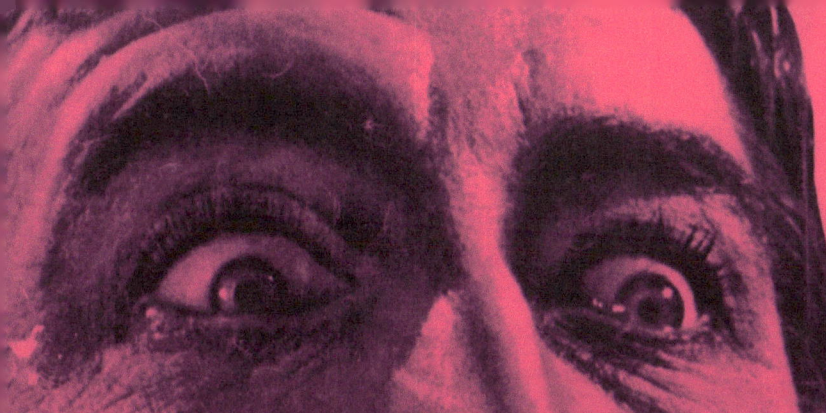

ALBUM OUT JULY 13!
GET IT ON ITUNES, AMAZON AND ALL FINE RECORD SHOPS

"Italian soundtrack funk that sounds like Goblin recording at Stax!"
-Wax Poetics Magazine

A killer combo of acclaimed indie rock musicians joined to recreate classic and obscure themes from 60s and 70s Italian film soundtracks.
Must hear! Must have!

MORE NEW TITLES ON NUBLU

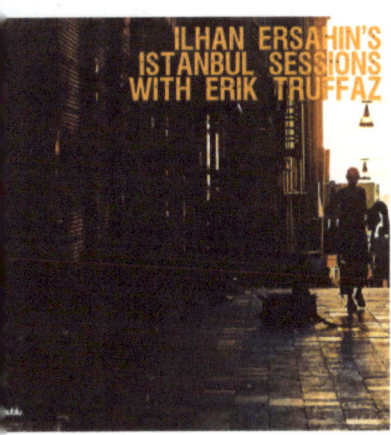

Ilhan Ersahin's
Istanbul Sessions with Erik Truffaz
CD / digital

Ilhan Ersahin
Bosphorus EP
Vinyl / digital

Hess is More
Democracy EP
Vinyl / digital

Photo by Josh Jensen.

The Bamboos
Antipodean funk band gets over Down Under

With greasy horn blasts and scratchy guitar licks, the Bamboos boast a seemingly authentic old-school sound that suggests their songs could have been recorded in Memphis or Detroit circa the '60s or '70s rather than in twenty-first-century Australia. The Melbourne-based octet have been traveling on an upward trajectory since their very first release—an obscure instrumental 45 called "Eel Oil"—was issued on their own Bamboo Shack imprint in 2001. Since then, the group hasn't looked back, and with three critically acclaimed albums under its belt for the U.K. label Tru Thoughts—*Step It Up* (2006), *Rawville* (2007), and *Side-Stepper* (2008)—they've steadily accrued an army of fans that includes DJs like funk fanatic Keb Darge.

Now they've upped the ante with a new album, *4*, which, according to Lance Ferguson—the Bamboos' New Zealand–born leader, producer, guitarist, and chief songwriter—is the group's best yet. "I wanted to take all the idiosyncrasies of the band and mold them into something that would make it instantly identifiable as a Bamboos record rather than a record aligned with any certain scene or sound," says Ferguson. "It's nearly ten years since our first single, so the music has changed a lot in that time, and now, for me, it's really all about just trying to write good songs. The previous albums have tipped their hats in various stylistic directions, and I wanted to pull these together into a cohesive whole. We had more time and a bigger budget to work with, so I was also able to go into much finer detail in the recording and mixing process."

Certainly, the new album is the group's most accessible offering yet, thanks mainly to the presence of ace vocalist Kylie Auldist, who, album by album, has progressively played a more prominent role. Ferguson—who also helmed Auldist's two solo albums, *Just Say* and *Made of Stone*—welcomes the chanteuse's bigger contribution to the band's sound. "She possesses a beautiful, soulful voice that is complemented by her unpretentious and down-to-earth nature," says Ferguson with enthusiasm. "Audiences really respond to the energy a live vocalist can bring, and it's also a real direct and personal connection when someone is singing to and for you. She is the perfect foil for seven guys sweating it out in suits onstage."

The Bamboos' main man also reveals that Auldist is now a permanent fixture in the band. "Though we have Lyrics Born and King Merc featuring on *4*, it was important for me to keep the guest vocalists to a minimum and make it clear that Kylie Auldist *is* the Bamboos' lead singer by featuring her on the majority of the songs," explains Ferguson. "I think with the next record, all the vocal duties will be taken care of exclusively by Kylie."

Though the Bamboos haven't ventured as far as the United States yet, Ferguson reveals that wheels are already in motion for an early 2011 U.S. tour. America, you have been warned.
● **Charles Waring**

FAT BEATS
UPCOMING RELEASES

Krs-One & True Master /// Meta-Historical [LP/CD]

August, 10th

Homeboy Sandman /// The Good Sun [2LP/CD]

June, 1st

DJ Muggs & Ill Bill /// Kill Devil Hills [2LP/CD]

August, 24th

Eternia & MoSS /// At Last [LP/CD]

June, 29th

Black Milk /// Album Of The Year [LP/CD]

September, 14th

Slum Village /// Fantastic, Vol. 2.10 [2LP/CD]

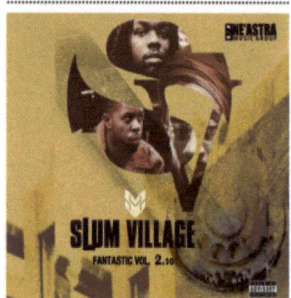

June, 8th

Pugs Atoms /// Kinda Like A Rapper [CD]

June, 1st

AG & Ray West /// Everything's Berri [CD]

June, 29th

Setenta /// Funky Tumbao [LP/CD]

June, 16th

WWW.FATBEATS.COM

VISIT OUR RETAIL STORES:
NEW YORK — 406 6th Ave, 2nd Floor, NY 10011 / 212.673.3883
LOS ANGELES — 7600 Melrose Ave, Suite J 2nd Floor, CA 90036 / 323.655.8997

FOR WHOLESALE ORDERS CALL: 718.875.8191

fatbeats

GO YOUR OWN WAY

digital.waxpoetics.com/converse

TITO RAMOS
"HEAVEN (IS NOT FOR EVERYONE)"
b/w BILAL "FREE"

Nine years ago, a dreadlocked vocalist named Bilal released a debut album that would drop him into the eye of what was being called the neo-soul movement; *1st Born Second* was lauded as a significant work in a subgenre the media was using to house male vocalists like D'Angelo and Maxwell. But as much attention as this threw onto Bilal, the Philadelphia native felt limited by the neo-soul tag and wasn't particularly interested in operating within its confines.

Now, in 2010, deeper into his career and moving past the 2006 shelving of *Love for Sale*—an album many consider to be one of the finest soul/R&B albums to *never* be released—Bilal looks back to where he was initially pigeonholed and actively stretches away from it.

"Free," appearing exclusively on wax for this installment of the Converse 45 series, acts as a precursor to the September release of his third album, *Airtight's Revenge*. Produced by Nottz, the track sees Bilal reaching for ideas outside of the neo-soul box. The edges are harder, the groove is tighter, and Bilal's lyrics aren't about love as much as life in general. Nottz lifts the beat from the Supremes' "Automatically Sunshine," and Bilal echoes Mary Wilson's sentiment (as written by Smokey Robinson): "No road is too rough to travel / We'll walk barefoot on life's gravel."

At a recent listening session for *Airtight's Revenge* in his current base of New York City, Bilal reflected that his concepts had progressed since the candles and baby oil of his 2000 single "Soul Sista." "Free" exemplifies this progression and gives us a good indication of where he's at—both musically and otherwise—right now.

Similarly, Tito "Big T" Ramos was at a significant point in his life back in 1972 when he released the album *Where My Head Is At* (in a nice synergy, this was also the release year of the Supremes 45 that Bilal draws from). This was the first time Ramos would stand alone as an artist, although he had been a name around his home of Spanish Harlem and on the Latin scene since the late '60s, lending his talent as a singer and writer to Johnny Colón's orchestra and his own TnT Band. His solo debut drew on sounds big at the time—mainly Motown and doo-wop—and on top of jazz riffs coupled with R&B and Latin vibes, Ramos was gravitating towards a strong spiritual connection with love.

The partying and drugs he engaged in with the TnT Band alongside friend and collaborator Tony Rojas had left its strain, and Ramos found clarity by stepping out and creating an album on his own. He put so much of himself into what surfaced as *Where My Head Is At*: every day for around six months, he wrote what he lived and lived what he wrote.

The opening track, "Heaven (Is Not for Everyone)," sees Ramos holding a mirror up to the listener's character, and asking them if they like what they see. "Take a look at yourself, and see where you belong," he sings vehemently. While the work Ramos did for Johnny Colón—like the classic "Boogaloo Blues"—had opened him up creatively, it wasn't until he broke away that he could really see who he was. In his own words, this was Ramos, and he was looking directly and unwaveringly at us, saying, "This is exactly *Where My Head Is At*." ● Marisa Aveling

---

*Subscriber copies of Wax Poetics Magazine are polybagged with an exclusive 45, presented by Converse. To subscribe, visit waxpoetics.com/subscribe. Offer available to U.S. subscribers while promotion lasts.

THE SHRINE

THE REBIRTH OF CHICAGO COOL

www.theshrinechicago.com

DAVE MULLER

Les Dogon *Les Chants de la Vie/Le Rituel Funéraire*
(Radiodiffusion de la France D'Outre-Mer) 1958

"For me, the single most reliable source of wonder is the French label Ocora. Their catalog contains field recordings of indigenous cultures from Africa to the Arctic. Sounds made not because someone wanted to make them, but because they had to make them, or because making music was as much a part of life as breathing. Before Ocora existed, Radiodiffusion de la France D'Outre-Mer released this double 10-inch in 1958. The Dogon, who live in the central plateau region of Mali, are documented from *Les Chants de la Vie* to *Le Rituel Funéraire*. Life and death are rendered on the stunning front cover. Bound with a plastic comb, the package contains sixteen pages of photos and detailed notes. And it's all in French, adding to the mystery."

Dave Muller was born in San Francisco in 1964 and currently lives and works in Los Angeles. He earned his BAS at the University of California, Davis, and his MFA from the California Institute of the Arts.

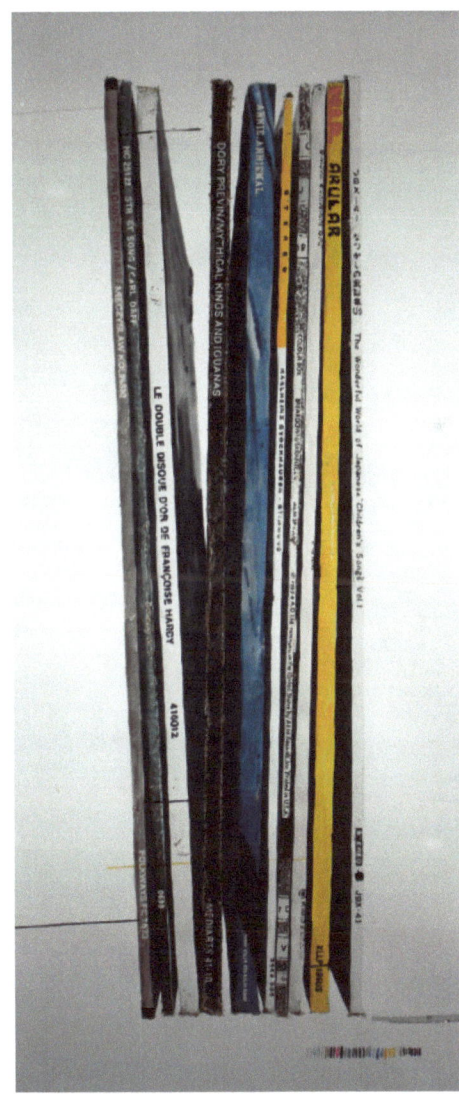

Dave Muller, *Dave's Top Ten (03/23/09: Muller Family Favorites)*, 2009. Acrylic on paper, framed, 86.5 × 38.5 inches. Courtesy of the artist and Blum & Poe, Los Angeles.

XAVIERA SIMMONS

Metallica ...And Justice for All (Elektra) 1988

"I live in New York City, so almost all of my friends produce brilliant music, and I love their records. Especially TV on the Radio, whose *Dear Science* would have been my top choice had I not been having a heavy-metal moment. Right now, I am excited about Metallica's *...And Justice for All*. Metallica is all I listen to while working in my studio lately. Well, besides D'Angelo's *Voodoo* and any records by Grace Jones, Cat Power, OutKast, Black Sabbath, Marvin Gaye, Bob Dylan, Rufus and Chaka Khan, Lenny Kravitz, My Morning Jacket, Max Roach (*Percussion Bitter Sweet*), A Tribe Called Quest, and the *Éthiopiques* collections. I love Metallica's in-your-face fierceness. Their music is restless, angsty, inspiring, frustrated, angry, perfectionist, and made-in-America soulful."

Xaviera Simmons was born in New York in 1974 and currently lives and works in Brooklyn. She earned her BFA in photography from Bard College in 2004 and completed the Whitney Museum Independent Study Program in 2005. She was the 2008 winner of the David C. Driskell Prize.

Xaviera Simmons, "Session One: Around the Y" from *Thundersnow Road*, North Carolina, 2010. Color photograph. Commissioned by the Nasher Museum of Art at Duke University. Courtesy of the artist.

DARIO ROBLETO

The Smiths *Meat Is Murder* (Rough Trade) 1985

"There are certain advantages to melancholy. A particular *creative potential* of melancholy. Every artist worth their weight must learn to harness that whale knowing they will be pulled under but always, undoubtedly, pulled back up too. It's when you break the surface that you better have the tools to shout what your heart's telling you. I first vaguely sensed this in the unlikeliest of places and seasons: Texas, summer, 1985, with the release of the Smiths' *Meat Is Murder*. It has now been twenty-five years of sorting out the ramifications of that day and every Smiths and Morrissey release since. *Meat Is Murder* is part of an unbroken whole that extends back millennia from Sappho, Rilke, Wilde, Dickinson, Holiday, and Cline."

Dario Robleto was born in San Antonio in 1972 and currently lives and works in Houston. He received his BFA from the University of Texas, San Antonio, in 1997 and in 1996 attended the Summer School of Music and Art at Yale University.

Dario Robleto, *Sometimes Billie Is All That Holds Me Together*, 1998–1999. Hand-ground and melted vinyl records, various clothing, acrylic, spray paint. Several new buttons were crafted from melted Billie Holiday records to replace missing buttons on found, abandoned, or thrift-store clothing. After the discarded clothing was made whole again, it was re-donated to the thrift stores or placed back where it was originally found. Dimensions variable. Collection of Rebecca and Alexander Stewart. Image courtesy of the artist and Kerry Inman Gallery, Houston. Photo by Ansen Seale.

STUDIO RUNDOWN

Bob Power remembers five spots that made history

by **Brad Farberman**

What's in a name? Well, no one's accusing Bob Power of false advertising. Since the mid-1980s, the esteemed producer and engineer has beefed up the recordings of everyone from D'Angelo to A Tribe Called Quest in efforts to make our world a doper-sounding place. And who better to do it than a cat named *Bob Power*?

Born in Chicago to a decidedly unmusical family in 1952, Bob Power relocated with his family to Rye, New York, when Bob was three. There, in close proximity to the Bronx, Power inherited his sister's guitar—she'd lost interest in "Blowin' in the Wind" by this point—and fell prey to the sounds of rock and roll and R&B.

"I was fourteen or fifteen in a friend's parents' living room, and they put on Otis *Live in Europe*," remembers Power. "And 'Try a Little Tenderness' on this recording…I get chills thinking about it. It brings down the house with, like, ten thousand people screaming his name. That was a real mindblower."

In 1970, Power left for St. Louis, where he would balance his theory and composition studies at Webster College with work in rock and soul bands at night. In '75, he took off for an eight-year stay in San Francisco—"like everybody does"—and fell into scoring, among other things.

"Because I had a background in composition, I got some gigs scoring television shows, which subsidized my playing jazz," says Power. "I was a journeyman musician just trying to work."

But the real work was in New York. Power made it back to the Apple in 1982, and soon after tried his hand at engineering. In 1985, while filling in for a coworker, Power mixed and recorded Stetsasonic's *On Fire*; it didn't take long until Tribe, De La, and a host of others came looking for Bob.

"No one told me it was gonna be like this," says Power. "No one told me I didn't have to wear a suit."

Deee-Lite "Groove Is in the Heart" (Elektra) 1990
Recorded by Bob Power at Calliope Studios, NYC

That was an incredible record. And they really were much more pivotal in usage of samples in pop music than most people give them credit for: Kier, Dmitri, [and] Towa, who was the first DJ I'd ever seen who had real slice-and-dice skills, and that blew my mind. He did some cuts on that that were like, "Wow!" And then I got to spend the weekend with Bootsy, which was fantastic. I did my undergrad in St. Louis, so there's Midwest things. And Bootsy's from Cincinnati. Certain food things, like chili mac—which is macaroni and chili—but it's a real Cincinnati thing. And we started riffin' about that. And I had played in these R&B circuits around the Midwest, so we just vibed. It was cool.

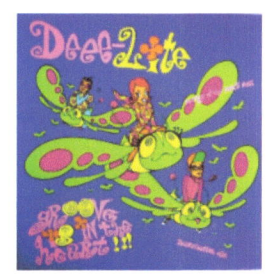

Me'Shell Ndegéocello *Plantation Lullabies* (Maverick) 1993
Produced, mixed, and recorded by Bob Power at Sorcerer Sound, NYC

Me'Shell is one of those people like D'Angelo. Like Joni Mitchell. Like Stevie Wonder. They come along and they make music in a way that is *completely* original. Her demos were ferocious. They were so good, but it wasn't quite a record. So that was a tough thing. We chased the demo on that. And I think I even sampled some stuff or flew some stuff in off the eight-track tapes from that. And she had people she wanted to work with, musicians and stuff like that. And she did a lot of stuff herself. I didn't have to make anything up for that. There was some creative give-and-take, but basically, it's: help this person get their vision down on tape.

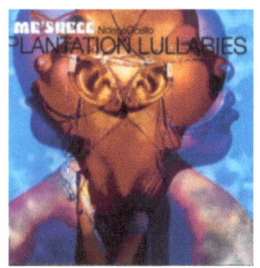

D'Angelo *Brown Sugar* (EMI) 1995
Produced, mixed, and recorded by Bob Power at Battery Studios, NYC

I did the first half of the album, and I ended up mixing the track "Brown Sugar" for Ali [Shaheed Muhammad]. So in the case of D, it was just a question of corralling that creative energy and making sure we got it onto tape. And making sure it was good but not too tidied up, because then it's not really true to who he is as an artist. So that was the challenge about that: how to make the downbeats match on the kick drums but leave all the other stuff that was all kind of rickety and had a little hitch in the beat. How to make it, "Okay, this sounds like a modern record, but it has all that flavor at the same time."

Chaka Khan *Epiphany: The Best of Chaka Khan, Volume One* (Reprise) 1996
Mixed by Bob Power at Enterprise Studios, Los Angeles

We mixed at the late, great Enterprise in L.A., and it was a great-sounding room—and the record sounds really incredible—but I think only a few tracks were released on a greatest hits album. And there are some tracks that are unreleased that are among the most incredible recordings I've ever heard. And mixing Chaka is a challenge, because her dynamic range as a singer is, like, from zero to 120, and you blink and you're at 120. I had to bring her vocal back on four or five different faders and switch between them, because the timbre of her voice in different registers was so different. I met Chaka and she punched me in the arm. "You that guy that made me sound good."

Erykah Badu "On & On" (Kedar Entertainment/Universal) 1997
Produced, mixed, and recorded by Bob Power at Battery Studios, NYC

[Label owner] Kedar [Massenburg] introduced me to Erykah, and the demo for that was fantastic. And I chased the demo. I'll be very honest about it. I definitely brought some things to it: there was no bridge in it, and I changed some of the instrumentation a little bit, and there were some samples that we couldn't use, so I actually recreated certain things like that. And you know, Erykah is a real artist. So with Erykah, you don't have to manufacture anything. And the funny thing is—and I say this with the utmost respect—her grand Afro-diva thing? She doesn't put that on. When I first met her, she had been teaching dance at a community center in Dallas, and she was exactly the same way.

On a recent afternoon in Hell's Kitchen, just up the block from—no joke—the Hit Factory Condominium, hard hats replaced the porkpie hats that used to congregate outside 460 West Fifty-fourth Street. On the plot where Sony Music Studios once stood, workers were erecting an eight-story luxury apartment complex. The master mixer and masterer Bob Power spent six years of his life on a site that now promises "top-of-the-line amenities" and "private cabanas."

"That was one of the greatest studios that ever existed," remembers Power. "There were six state-of-the-art, world-class rooms at Sony, and the personnel there was far and away some of the best people in the world in their different areas. The Fugees worked a lot there. Michael Jackson block-booked one of the rooms for almost a year once, and they cordoned off the whole end of the facility."

J
Tenth, men loaded gear into Avatar Studios, the spot where the   . Power
spe

"I did a jazz record with Me'Shell there that I recorded and coproduced, and that thing sounds really, really good," says Pov   *The Spirit Music Jami* "She hired very idiosyncratic musicians and then put them in unusual settings and

But Power's career as a producer and engineer started farther downtown, on a particularly filthy stretch of New York's Garment District known as Thirty-seventh Street between Seventh and Eighth. There, among a seemingly infinite number of bars and discount clothing stores, sat Calliope Studios, may it rest in peace.

"In '85, I had been working out of a studio called Calliope, which ended up being a very seminal hip-hop studio," says Power. "And the owner would fall asleep at the console at six in the morning, 'cause I used to work overnight. And I'd finish off the mix myself."

It was also at Calliope that Power first demonstrated a natural aptitude for mixing and recording hip-hop.

"If you think about the first wave of hip-hop, with real 808s that came out of the box, it was pretty clear to me right away, that low end," says Power. "And also Tip standing over my shoulder saying, 'More, more, more!'"

Around 1989, Power also started working at a space in Chelsea, on West Twenty-fifth Street. At the now-defunct Battery Studios, Power tricked out tracks by D'Angelo, A

"The Roots are—and I say this benevolently, and with love—the most wonderful example of creative anarchy you could ever imagine," says Power. "Often, I would work on something for a couple of days, and then Ahmir would come in and say, 'Oh, did you get those other drums?' And I'm like, 'What other drums?' 'Oh, there's a two-inch tape. It'll come up from Philly.

*EPA-estimated 29 city/40 hwy/33 combined mpg, automatic SFE. Class is Compact Cars vs. 2010 competitors. Fiesta SES shown. EPA-estimated 29 city/38 hwy/33 combined mpg, automatic.

Twenty-seventh Street. At Chez Bob, just a stone's throw from where Battery used to be, he's worked on projects by Me'Shell, Keziah Jones, J Dilla, and Carlos Niño and Miguel Atwood-Ferguson.

"I didn't do it by design, but having my own room—and having it turn out to be sonically an incredibly accurate room, and always having had enough of my own gear to sink a boat—it's dovetailed nicely with the movement with mixers," says Power. "And pretty much mixers all have their own rooms now. Even though I've mixed in the same rooms a lot, my chair and my monitors are in *exactly* the same place every day. My whole level of aural engagement and how I hear things is enhanced about twenty times what it used to be five years ago."

Believe the hype. After all this time, Power's ears are still growing at an alarming rate. Stranger still, the word at NYU is he's contemplating a side gig as a director.

"I often say to students, 'We're not making a documentary, we're making a film,'" says Power. "There's a term I use on mixing and recording: 'Better than real.' And that's one of the cool things about the recording process. If you're really lucky, the _____ *better*. Like a film, it's cooler than it is if you just saw the same thing on the street."

40 HWY **MILES PER GALLON.**
TAKES YOU SO MANY PLACES.

INTRODUCING THE NEW **FIESTA**
The most fuel-efficient car of its kind.* **It's a pretty big deal.**

fordvehicles.com

Ford

Drive one.

Funky Beatitude

Melvin Bliss's "Synthetic Substitution" helped pattern the sound of hip-hop

by **Angus Batey**

Photo by Matt Rogers.

It's a balmy summer day in 2004, and Kool Keith, the idiosyncratic, ultra-magnetic MC, is enjoying a reverie. The subject under discussion is the early days of his group, who helped transform New York rap in the early part of the music's golden age; and while Keith's prowess on the mic dominates, there's also a need to talk about the samples that helped him and his bandmates create this new aesthetic.

We're in a hotel in London's financial district that's built on the site of the infamous Bedlam, the seventeenth-century Bethlehem Hospital, which started out as a brutal prototype of a mental institution, and turned into a grim carnival-sideshow attraction, with on-the-take staff conducting tours of the inmates for paying visitors. So Keith, with his Bellevue shtick and propensity for logic-leaps and lyrical non sequiturs, seems on home turf. In a few minutes, he'll be on the Tube—London's sweltering subway—heading to Chinatown in search of a meal, and complaining about how the neo-soul movement ruined hip-hop, as it "takes away from rap itself. It takes away from the Just-Ice. It takes away from the Tricky T. It takes away from the Eric B. and the EPMD." But for now, he's digging deep in his memory crates, trying to explain where the Ultramagnetic MC's got that *other* sound from. There's only one place to start.

"I was listening to 'I Know You Got Soul,'" he begins—though, later, his Ultra cohort, Ced Gee, will say that Keith is mistaken, and the Eric B. & Rakim track in question was in fact "Eric B. Is President." "And I said to Ced, 'You know, we

Photo courtesy of Melvin Bliss.

day. But when we got there, the show had just ended. She was sitting with her hands folded on the bar and her head down on her hands. So the owner said, 'Hey, Billie, can these sailors come in and say hello to you?' And she said, 'Bring the sailor boys in!' So we went over to her, and she said, 'I'm sorry you boys missed the show. What's your favorite song?' At that time, of course—this was either in '56 or '57—we said 'God Bless the Child.' Do you know? Billie Holliday lifted her head up off the bar and sang 'God Bless the Child,' with no music or nothin'. It was amazing."

In 1957, Seaman Second Class McClelland found himself in New York, and entered the amateur-hour talent show at the Apollo Theater in Harlem. He got up in his white uniform and sang "the song Roy Hamilton had just came out with, 'You'll Never Walk Alone.' I won four weeks in a row with that song. Bobby Schiffman Jr., who was the son of the owner of the Apollo, asked me when I was getting out of the Navy. I said, 'Well, I'm getting out next year.' And he said, 'If you come back to New York, I'll manage you.' So that's what happened."

The business relationship wasn't a long one, but the young man began to make a name for himself in the city's numerous jazz clubs. He did stints as the house singer at Birdland where he sang with Max Roach, Yusef Lateef, and Art Blakey. He worked the same stages as comedians like Flip Wilson and Redd Foxx. He'd found lodgings in a hotel popular with musicians opposite Birdland, at Broadway and Fifty-second Street; Big Maybelle lived down the hallway for a while. But when it came to haircuts, Melvin would travel uptown, to a barbershop around the corner from the Apollo, at 125th Street and Seventh Avenue.

"I think it was called the Alhambra," Bliss says. "All the celebrities would go there. Jackie Wilson and James Brown both got their hair done there, and Nat King Cole. You'd have, like, nine or ten barbers, and while you were waiting, we'd ask Nat questions and talk to him, or he'd talk and everyone would just shut up and listen. In those days, the big stars could do things like that. You didn't have paparazzi chasing people like they do nowadays in Hollywood—everybody respected everybody."

But the fame and fortune enjoyed by those he hung out with continued to elude Melvin. He stayed in New York, working the jazz clubs, spending the '60s pitching for any work as a professional singer he could get, alternating paying gigs with short-lived non-music jobs. "I've had different jobs though my life, to survive," he says. "But as soon as I get one, it lasts two weeks. I tell them I've gotta go and do a concert; they tell me I can't go, and I quit."

Rather than wait for fame to come knocking, he tried to take charge. Which is why, one day in 1972, he found himself at a venue in Queens, waiting to speak to the manager about renting it, so he could promote his own concert. While hanging around, he started talking to a woman and told her he was a singer. "And she says, 'Oh, that's wonderful—my son is a songwriter with a group called the Exciters, and he's looking for a singer for a song he's written.'" Numbers were exchanged, and a couple of days later, he was on the phone with the writer, Herb Rooney.

"I went to his home, and he just had a guitar there, and started playing the riffs and the rhythms of the song," Melvin recalls of "Reward." "I liked it, and he liked the little tryout that I did, so we got together in the studio." Bliss had only recorded once before, years earlier—a track called "Hello," for a compilation that, as far as he knows, was never released. So when Rooney suggested turning that first demo into a single, it was a chance not to be passed up. Rooney and Melvin ran down a list of possible pseudonyms, settling on Bliss for the simple reason that the singer "liked it—it was short, and very, very nice, you know?"

Contracts were signed, and studio time for Melvin to record "Reward" was booked. As an afterthought, Rooney gave Bliss a cassette with a demo of another song that he'd decided would be the B-side. "I was enveloped by the rhythm," Bliss says of his first reaction to "Synthetic Substitution." "It was exciting, and just very, very *strange*. I had to put myself into it, because it was so different to anything I'd ever done."

The sessions took place on the fourth or fifth floor of the building on West Fifty-fourth Street that would later house, in its basement, the iconic Studio 54. Bliss took several takes to nail his part. The music had been recorded earlier—Rooney, who was producer as well as writer, supervised those sessions alongside arranger Bert Keyes (who also worked on Skull Snaps' breakbeat classic, "It's a New Day"). Bliss, who was only around to record his vocals, was never sure of the identities of the musicians—apart from one. The drums, which would eventually go on to fuel so many hip-hop classics, were played by Bernard Purdie. "Told you I'd been around some big people!" Bliss chuckles. "All the paperwork's long gone, and nobody's got any record of the credits. But I'm absolutely sure the beat is Bernard Purdie."

And what about that enigmatic song? What does the man who recorded it think about it today?

"The gist of the song is about things that are synthetic, meaning unreal," Bliss begins. "The story line is about phoniness and unrealism. The world was in disarray, and everything around was unbelievable: everything was confusion and chaos,

everything was uncertain, everything was questioned. I think 'Synthetic Substitution' would have been perfect for the play *Hair*, it was in that same genre of life."

The record did well enough, getting on playlists in Europe and selling reasonably in the U.S. But the parent label, Opel, which was set to bankroll a slate of recordings on the new Sunburst imprint, fell apart. Bliss's recording career was over before it had properly begun. Bliss went back to the jazz clubs of New York, and, apart from a brief stint co-owning a bar on the Caribbean island of St. Martin, that's where he's remained ever since. He's expanded his range a bit, learning Hebrew phonetically so he can play bar mitzvahs, and adding some Tony Bennett and Rat Pack songs to a repertoire that already included a Nat King Cole tribute segment. "I sing in Yiddish, I do the top-hat thing, I do jazz, swing," he says. "Everything—just to stay alive." A self-financed CD, *Mix It Up*, was recorded in 2001, mainly to sell at shows. It is still available from the online store CD Baby.

Bliss had forgotten all about "Reward," never mind "Synthetic Substitution," until his son told him that the 45 was attracting high prices in online auctions, due to its status as a revered sample source. "I have a little age on me, so I didn't even know there was hip-hop!" he laughs. "I haven't seen a cent from any of this. An attorney was gonna look into it to see if she could get me some royalties, but she wanted money up front, and I couldn't afford to do the research." Various proposals to rerecord the track have come to nothing. "But I'd love to collaborate with any of the hip-hop artists today," he says. "Please put that in the article!"

A second album is in the planning stages, though as yet, there's nothing complete other than the title. "It's going to be called *Down Here on the Ground*," Bliss says. "That was one of Wes Montgomery's favorite songs, and Lou Rawls also recorded it." And "Synthetic Substitution" is at last earning a few dollars for its creator, as Bliss has reissued the track as a digital download.

Sometimes, it's as if songs have a life, then sampling gives them an afterlife. This has certainly been the case for "Synthetic Substitution," though the fact that its maker has seen so little evidence of that ghostly echo makes this particular saga ring a little bit hollow.

"I have a mixed reaction to [sampling]," Bliss says. "I'm glad that people like it, but I feel annoyed, because I haven't gotten my due, honestly. I would just like to get a little money under my belt from it—maybe get some work out of it, some appearances, some traveling. I'm not bitter about it, but if there's record companies out there makin' money from it, I should be getting some money from somewhere, right?" ○

ACADEMY RECORDS PRESENTS.....

Available Soon!

Out Now!

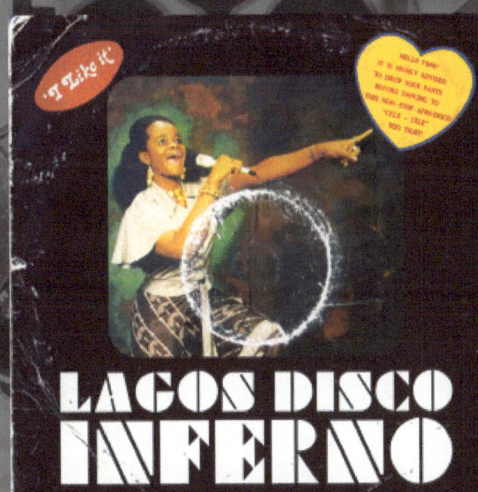

PSYCHEDELIC ALIENS
'Psycho African Beat' is the complete recorded output of this amazing Ghanian group circa '69 - '70. The Alien's unprecedented music blends American funk, soul, garage rock and psych with African rhythms and melodies.

LAGOS DISCO INFERNO
12 Red Hot Slices from the Golden Age of Nigerian Disco, '74 - '81

Coming soon! Raw Psychedelic Funk from Ghana!

THIS IS MARIJATA
MARIJATA
SIMIGWA

In Stores Now!

OFEGE
SJOB MOVEMENT
MEBUSAS

Academy Records & CDS
12 West 18th ST NYC 10011
212-242-3000
Academy_Records.Com

Academy Records
415 East 12th St NYC 10009
212-780-9166
Academylps.Com

Academy Annex
96 North 6th St Brooklyn 11211
718-218-8200
AcademyAnnex.Com

SISTER SANCTIFIED

Funkstress Erykah Badu enlightens from a higher ground

by **Travis Atria**

There are a few things to know about Erykah Badu. First, she lives on a different plane. One that only true-blue, dyed-in-the-wool artists inhabit. From the moment she hit with 1997's *Baduizm*, it was clear that this lithe woman with the high headdress belonged to a different class. Critics said she sang like Billie Holiday, which she did and she didn't. Her music wasn't hip-hop, and it wasn't soul, and it wasn't R&B, so they had to invent a term: neo-soul. Former Motown president Kedar Massenburg, who discovered Badu, coined that term to describe her and a movement of similar artists like D'Angelo and Lauryn Hill.

Second thing is, she's weird. This is a woman who once said her fantasy man is Batman and that the concept of time is for White people. But she's weird in the way that Einstein was weird, and the way that Prince is weird, and the way that all people who possess creative genius are weird.

Third, she is confident and charming as hell. Badu knows that songs like "Tyrone" have inspired a generation of women, and albums like *Mama's Gun* have changed the musical landscape. She knows that her fashion sense, spiritual beliefs, and music videos—which she directs herself—resonate with millions of people. And she's okay with that.

Our conversation is punctuated by the laughter of her children in the background, a reminder that Badu is a mother on top of everything else. In the middle of her first answer, Badu pauses and says, "*Wax Poetics* is one of my favorite magazines ever. You know how people used to have *Jet* magazine spread on their table? I got all the *Wax Poetics* covers." Maybe she's being serious, or maybe it's just part of the charm. The performer laying it on thick. But then again, Badu isn't known for glad-handing. Part of her success is due, no doubt, to the fact that she is brutally honest, especially in her music. In March, Badu released *New Amerykah Part Two: Return of the Ankh*. It is the second volume documenting a creative wet season during which Badu was working with producers like Madlib and Karriem Riggins and writing several songs a day.

A few themes come up a lot when researching your life and career. One is duality. You are a mother and a musician. Your music is part hip-hop and part soul. You have a real name and a stage name. Your stage name, Erykah, has the Egyptian symbol "ka" in it, which refers to a spiritual double. What's your take on that?

I'm a Pisces. I guess there are two sides of me. There's a little girl, and there's a very, very old woman. No in-between. A little naïve girl and a very wise old woman.

Other artists—like Questlove, Common, Andre 3000, D'Angelo, and Jill Scott—play a large role in your life. And most of those artists came up with you in the so-called neo-soul movement. What is the state of that movement now?

I think that it still exists. We are still here. We are still multiplying. *Mama's Gun* set many children out in the world, and I see them manifesting whatever it is. I don't know what it's called,

(*previous spread*) Photo by Kenneth Cappello, courtesy of Motown/Universal. (*right*) Photo by Bode Helm, courtesy of Motown/Universal.

what the movement is called. To me, it's the funk movement, you know? That's what it is to me—it's the funk. They called it neo-soul, but they mistitled it. I would rather be neo-funk. It's the thing we all have, and a lot of us who you named, our music doesn't sound alike, really. We use musicians in common, which makes us sound alike, but we have totally different viewpoints and come from different places, musically. I think what we have in common is that thang, and it has an *a* in it. It's a thang that you can't really put your finger on. It's a DNA thang.

I agree that you don't sound alike, but one thing you all have in common is a deep knowledge of music, soul and R&B music in particular. You are on the cutting edge of hip-hop, but you also know where hip-hop came from.

We all know that hip-hop is people. We are hip-hop. And another thing is we have a same kind of—I don't know—it's a tribe almost. A foundation. We all collect records. We love music. We are serious about it. We do it whether we get paid or not. We collect wax. We share it. We are all, I feel, very giving when it comes to our art—selfishly giving—and very honest. Those are all the elements I see that we have in common.

Hair is another theme that runs through your career. For Black artists especially, it seems like hair has always been more than just a stylistic thing. It implies a deeper statement, from dreads to Afros and beyond.

It's a political statement.

And when you first came out, you had the headdress, later the big Afro, and a few changes in between. You seem to have a clear idea of the symbolism of hair.

Can I ask you a question before I answer it?

Of course.

I see different singers and musicians changing their hair all the time. Why is it such a big deal when I do it? What makes it a bigger event? Because everybody wants to know what she going to do with her hair next?

Well, to me, those artists are doing it from a stylistic perspective. But I get the sense that you put more thought into it than that. Maybe not. I just wanted to find out.

You know what? It's just where I am at the time. I think it has meaning for all of us. I change it often, and what's common with it is that it's all natural. I've never changed the texture of it or put chemicals on it to change what that is. To me, my hair is my antenna. I feel like I'm getting some kind of signals through these follicles.

There's even biblical significance to it. Samson's power was in his hair.

Yeah, but I guess my power is in my belief more than in my hair. And those statements are just for you to enjoy aesthetically. Hair plays a great part in having a platform and choosing to be a recording artist. There once was no such thing as video. There was only an album cover. When I'm walkin' and dressin', I'm thinking about album covers that I looked at. There was no misunderstanding what this artist was going to do today or tomorrow, because the album covers said it all. That's all you had. That's who they were. This one white leather suit with rhinestones on it is all you gon' get for a while until something else come out. And it told the story of the whole album—where they were, who they were in time, how they felt, how cool they were, how cool they weren't. All I know about Bootsy is he's a cool motherfucker, because look what he got on. To me, that's the art of illusion when it comes to having this platform as an artist. You can create any kind of persona you want, and it means so much to me to be able to change that focus from time to time.

The new album is subtitled *Return of the Ankh*. What's the significance of the ankh?

The ankh has been the staple in my music since 1997. In *Baduizm*, the ankh is on the CD itself. In 1997, when it came out, I was wearing an ankh on my hand, and I had a tattoo painted on my shoulder. Millions of women after that had ankhs tattooed on their bodies because of the simple meaning. And they knew the meaning because when I came out with *Live* that same year, in November, I explained exactly what it was. On that album, it explains that an ankh is an ancient Kemetic word that means life. It means eternal life. It means the return to life. That word means all of those things. It means being sad, it means being full of joy, it means being afraid. It's just a word that encompasses all of those emotions in one. I just thought it was important. By that time, in November, I had grown very close to the audience, because I didn't even know I had a style or nothing until I got a record deal. But by that time, I wanted to share everything I had learned. I figured, "Hey, this is a platform." And I took that responsibility very seriously. The

reason why this album is called *Return of the Ankh* is because it's a reminder of that. Let's go back to when I was just Erykah Badu who just came out with a head wrap, and there were no preconceived notions. There was no pointing fingers. It was all about the music. It was all about the music and the love and the intention.

I read that you worked with several underground hip-hop producers for *Return of the Ankh*, like Madlib and Karriem Riggins. Who else did you work with, and how did it affect the album?

Oh, you haven't did your research, huh? You going to make me do all the work, Travis. Well, *New Amerykah Part One* and *Two* is two parts of the same place I was in. *Part One* is the left-brain feeling of where I was. Listen to *New Amerykah Part One*—it's social, analytical, political, psychoanalytical. *Part Two* is the very emotional part of it, the inner me. The little-girl me. *Part One* is the woman me. The elder.

I did read about that.

You did read that. [*laughs*]

I'm just wondering how did these different producers change the outcome?

I'm long-winded. I'm getting to it. [*laughs*] Madlib is my friend and so is Dilla and so is Karriem Riggins, the drummer and producer. And so is the group Sa-Ra, who is also on the project. Georgia Anne Muldrow, who is also on the project. Jah Born, who did "On and On" and "On and On Part Two," who is also on the project. And this new dude I just met through some cats in L.A.; his name is Ta'Raach. He's also on the project. And of course Questlove and James Poyser, who is a staple in my music.

Poyser's name comes up a lot in your work.

Yeah, that's my studio husband. We finish each other's musical statements and sentences. He's my beloved friend and companion, musically. I did all these songs between 2003 and 2008 or 2009, because I had just come out of what people call writer's block. *Worldwide Underground* was the process of trying to come out of that. But what I found out is that there's no such thing as writer's block. It's just a downloading period—a time when you're supposed to be learning, moving, procrastinating, creating, making mistakes, and fixing them, so you have some inspiration. It was a data-gathering time. I hope no artist feels that they have writer's block, because they can probably psych themselves into thinking that that's what it is. And they won't get the lessons that they're supposed to get during that time [because they're] so busy being worried about writer's block or creative block. There's no such thing. I'm a witness to that. When I found that out, I was relieved, and music started flowing out of me like a waterfall. I was moving so fast that I didn't have time to compose music, so I started taking tracks that I admired from different friends of mine—like Madlib—and put it right in GarageBand. And I'm writing four songs a day off of Madlib's mixtape beats, and I'm writing three songs a day from Dilla's mixtapes that I've had since they were cassette tapes. And then I get on iChat and I'm talking to different people—Q-Tip and Mos Def and everybody— "Send me some tracks, y'all. Send me tracks. I'm writing my ass off here. Give me some tracks." The more tracks they sent, the more I wrote and wrote and wrote. I did all this in GarageBand, and by the time it was over, I had so many songs. I want to say in the fifties or sixties. Every time I tell this story, the number gets bigger. I had seventy-nine songs….

[*laughs*] Hundreds.

Yeah, 176 songs. I had so much to say, and I split it in two pieces. I could have split it in four pieces, but I decided to split it in two pieces. There may be a *New Amerykah Part Three*. You never know, because there's just so much left from that stuff. So much beautiful residue, sweet smellin'. And my album artwork, man, is amazing. I think that's what *Wax Poetics* is about too. Just the classic pieces. I think I really met my visual artistic husband too. His name is Emek, and he is a rock poster artist, among other things. We worked together for the past seven years. He's the one that I want to represent me. The name of the piece of art on the front cover is called *Out My Mind, Just in Time*. It's a piece that the girl is covered in armor. She doesn't want her heart to be broken ever again, so she will never open it up again, and she has a hard shell around her. And something happens, and a paradigm shift begins to occur, some event and circumstance. And if you listen to *New Amerykah Part Two*, you'll hear these events and circumstances unfold. *Part One* talks about the hardening, how she became petrified. *Part Two* talks about the opening. How the layers come off.

The way you came out of that writer's block is interesting. You did the Frustrated Artist Tour in 2003. Is live performance a creative experience for you rather than just singing songs that are already written?

It's actually therapy to me. The stage is like a couch. It gives me a chance to close my eyes and get it all out, vibrationally. I focus it into good energy, because I don't want to push out a lot of bad stuff or good stuff on anybody. I want people to have they own shit. I just focus it into positive energy to be used for however. And for some reason, the audience and me and the band become one living organism, breathing back and forth. That's how I imagine it. It feels that way. It looks that way. And when we all leave, we leave satisfied. And I'm standing on the stage until I feel like that. ⊙

Travis Atria is a musician and writer based in Gainesville, Florida.

"The most innovative latin / funk album since the days of Santana, War and Fania"

EL EXISTENTIAL

Grupo Fantasma

IN STORES NOW

NatGeoMusic.net | GrupoFantasma.com

V.A. - PARTY-KELLER Vol. 3

CPT 355-1/-2/-3 (2LP/CD/digital)
release date: July 16th 2010

01. Peter Giger & Family Of Percussion "Here Comes The Family"
02. Richard Strauss "2001" (C.F. Peters Corp. Version)
03. Bronx River Parkway "La Valla"
04. The Delta Rhythm Section "King Midnite"
05. Quiller "Quiller"
06. Gizelle Smith "June"
07. Gino Dentie "Express"
08. Bo Kirkland & Ruth Davis "We Got The Recipe"
09. Ralph Marco Band "High Snobiety"
10. Special Touch "This Party Is Just For You"
11. Dizzy K Falola "Take It To The DJ"
12. B.A.Baracus Band "Mama Said Knock You Out"
13. Gino Dentie "Movin'"
14. Matrix 5 "Bicentennial Boogie"
15. Rahmlee "Down In Storyville"
16. Nazz "Loosen Up"

Here comes the 3rd chapter of the legendary funk-boogie-disco-rare groove compilation series compiled by Florian Keller

www.myspace.com/compostrecords

V.A. - ELASTE Vol. 3

AVANTGARDISTIC, GALACTIC SOUNDING COSMIC DISCO, PROTO-TECHNO, ELECTRONIC NEW WAVE AND CHEESY SLOW MOTION POP
COMPILED BY DOMPTEUR MOONER
CPT 347-1/-2/-3 (2LP/CD/digital)
OUT NOW!!!

The LAST POET

Gil Scott-Heron is still the first name on the rhyme scene

by **Patrick Sisson**

Gil Scott-Heron doesn't suffer no fools. During an afternoon phone call from his office in New York, the sixty-one-year-old author and performer fielded interview questions with the same combination of humor, bluntness, and insight that have made his poetry, novels, and lyrics so valued and influential over the last four decades. When asked about his relationship with hip-hop, he replied, "I haven't seen hip-hop lately. I see rappers as individuals." While I was trying to ferret out information about his forthcoming book, *The Last Holiday*, he told me he has 628 pages right now, and while he'd love to talk about each and every one of them, he'll let everyone read the book themselves. Towards the end of our conversation, he said, "I told you everything except my DNA. Don't you think you have enough for a story?"

His patience may have been tested, but his capacity for storytelling was barely tapped. Born in Chicago and raised in Tennessee and the Bronx, Scott-Heron's literary ambitions and social conscience quickly manifested themselves. After writing a novel, *The Vulture*, in 1968 at age nineteen, Scott-Heron began a long musical career with the release of *Small Talk at 125th and*

Lenox in 1970. He's collaborated with musicians such as Brian Jackson and Malcolm Cecil and industry legends like Bob Thiele and Clive Davis. The influence of his blend of sociopolitical commentary and R&B—as heard in seminal tracks like "The Bottle" and "The Revolution Will Not Be Televised"—has never waned and is in fact considered a key element in the evolution of hip-hop. But Scott-Heron's recent recorded output was sparse until the release of *I'm New Here*, which came out earlier this year. A set of modern tracks paired with the poet's frank observations, it was a pet project of XL Recordings' owner Richard Russell that found its genesis in Russell's 2006 visit to see Scott-Heron at Rikers Island, where the artist was serving time for cocaine possession. Scott-Heron's baritone voice may have aged, but his focus and literary integrity will never go out of style.

Tell me about growing up with your grandmother in Tennessee, which you discuss on the first track of the new album. How did she influence you?
She didn't have much of a formal education. She was a firm believer that you needed to have one of those if you want to know something. Her own children all graduated from college with honors, so there was a firm desire to get an education and to read. She had a big library in Tennessee, and I spent a lot of time in it.

Any books from that time that really influenced you?
I read a lot of Langston Hughes. He had a newspaper column in the *Chicago Defender*, the *Amsterdam News*, and all the Black papers. We were subscribers to the *Defender*. I think we paid twenty-five cents a week. It was actually a big influence.

When you moved to New York City later in your life, you wrote a paper about Langston Hughes, right?
Yeah, he was a reporter downtown working for the *New York Post*. He was giving a speech, and I was able to go down to see him. I got a tape recorder and recorded him and wrote a paper from what he spoke about. I wanted to be a writer from the time I was eleven. That's what I told everyone. You decide you want to be an astronaut or baseball player. I wanted to be a writer.

What is it about the work of guys like Jean Toomer and Langston Hughes that really spoke to you?
Langston was very literate and wrote all kinds of different things, but he had a sense of humor. I think a lot of people at that particular time didn't have much of a sense of humor. People were angry and outrageous, and the fact that he managed to maintain his sense of humor impressed me, because I think it's one of our most important senses.

That's something that's reflected in all your work, like

(previous spread and right)
Photo by Chuck Stewart.

"'B' Movie," the track about Reagan.
Of course, it's a big part of being a human being. If you've lost your sense of humor, I think you've lost your sense of humanity. It connects me to some of the people I most admire, people who either mixed comedy with art or art with comedy, people like Dick Gregory or Richard Pryor. They had a point to make, they tried to make some improvements, and humor was the foundation of it. You can't just start screaming at everybody. Everybody knows there are things wrong with this planet. But in order to make it through all the things that are going to happen to you in your life, you need to maintain humor. It's the most important aspect of yourself.

Was that really important to you when you were in prison?
Well, yeah, it's been important to me all my life. Not just in prison but everywhere else. I was in prison for having twenty dollars' worth of cocaine. If I was in any other Western country, I would have been given community service, a fine, or a ticket and told to get on out of the way.

How did you occupy your time, and what did you take out of the experience of being in prison?
I did a lot of reading. I did a lot of writing. I did a lot of studying and had a chance to catch up with myself. You sort of resolve yourself to it. You see, I had to confess to the crime to go on tour. They let me out to do a tour in Europe, and I came back and had to report to them.

When you were in prison, did anyone say to you, "Hey, you're Gil Scott-Heron, you wrote 'The Bottle.' What are you doing here on a drug charge?"
They asked what I was doing in prison at all, and I said time. Like, twenty dollars' worth of cocaine doesn't mean I'm the next one to go on methadone. Look at Robert Downey Jr. There are a whole lot of people with problems. It's when you get caught and what you get caught with, not that you got caught. Did you ever smoke reefer?

Yeah.
Ever get caught with it?

Not yet.
Yeah, see, same thing. There was a time when getting caught with a bit of reefer would have landed you in jail. So I'm saying that I got caught with what I got caught with, and I got put in jail. It was me instead of someone else.

How did you meet up with Brian Jackson and many of the other guys in the Midnight Band while at Lincoln University?
I was working with a vocalist named Victor Brown. We did different things around campus at coffee shops, and I was writing a song for him one day in a practice room. And Brian was in a room next to the one we were occupying. I told Vic,

   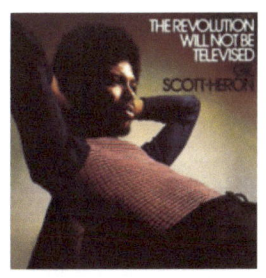
  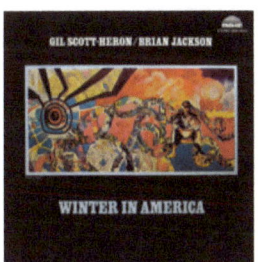 

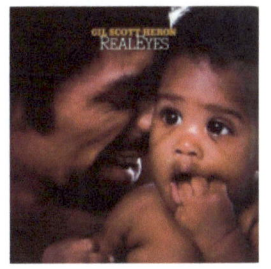   

"There's the guy I've seen playing around here. You need him as a piano player." I introduced him to Vic, and he worked with him for a while on a few other tunes. Brian told me that he had some compositions that would work well with lyrics, and we talked about it, and we got together. The first couple of things he brought to me worked out really well. I ended up with a recording contract, and Brian was a musician, so he was included with the sessions that we got to do with Bob Thiele.

How did the composition process work with you guys?
Music always came first. Brian would work on a composition, we'd talk about what he was thinking about when he wrote it, and I would try to work from that.

Why do you think you two worked together so well?
There have been far more prolific partnerships than ours, but we worked well together. The songs were unusual. They came from someone with a jazz and classical background, and a writer who appreciated those same influences.

At that time, or throughout your career, did you ever feel like you had a big message to broadcast to people?
Every songwriter you talk to feels like they have a message. I don't think I had more of a message than anybody else. I thought I was a better writer than some. The question is whether or not you're successful.

Before you recorded 1974's *Winter in America*, you moved down to Washington, D.C., with Brian and some of the guys in the band. Why did you make the move?
I went down there to teach. I was teaching creative writing, poetry, fiction, and composition at the University of D.C., after I left Baltimore, where I got my master's at Johns Hopkins. Brian came down, and we continued to work together.

How did the city and maybe the surroundings influence what you wrote on *Winter in America*? Were there specific people you were thinking of when you were writing these songs?
Yeah, "The Bottle" came from some folks who had gathered out in the parking lot near where I was staying. They'd gather in this parking lot and trade in the bottles they'd collected the previous night. A guy running a liquor store would open the back and give them what they wanted. I went out there to talk to them a couple times to see who they were and what they were doing, and I met some of their friends. It was fascinating, in all seasons, under all conditions, that those people would be there. I was fascinated by their dedication.

Who were they, what did they do?
One had been a doctor. Abortions were illegal in those days, but he had done a couple of them, and somebody told on him, and he lost his license. And when he lost his license, he lost his wife, and she took the children. He didn't know how to get his license back, and he lost his life. Somebody had begged him to do it and then ratted him out for performing the operation. One lady had worked for social services and saw someone she was trying to help overdose. She felt like everything she was doing didn't mean anything, everyone she was working with was a tragic figure, and she couldn't take it anymore. One guy was an air traffic controller who had misdirected a flight. He had two Navy jets on his screen. One was directed to lower its altitude and it lowered into the side of a mountain, and four people were killed.

No one set out to be an alcoholic. All of them had something happen in their lives that turned them around. This was right at the time when doctors were starting to determine that alcoholism and drug addiction was an illness, not just a social feeling or something weak about your character. It struck me that something needed to be done to help these people, not just jump on down on them like that.

***Winter in America* was about a dark period, and we're in a pretty dark period in America now. Do you feel things have gotten better nowadays?**
Of course they have. I mean, you know, things change. America was in a dark period, because all people who had been trying to do something positive had been lost: both of the Kennedys, Malcolm X, Martin Luther King Jr., Medgar Evers; all those people had been killed. We were trying to say that's how you get to winter. You put out the lights. People who were trying to bring sunshine to us had been extinguished.

Part of your critique at that time—that America was becoming a consumer, not a producer, and we needed to change—is still pretty timely.
We needed and need to change our perspectives on other countries. America is very arrogant, very obnoxious. We have so much arrogance. We haven't been around for that long, and we're trying to kick around countries that have been around for thousands of years. That seems to be very prominent in what's happening to us. We were admired by everyone, then there was a certain point where the arrogance overruled what people liked about us.

How did Clive Davis enter the picture?
He just entered the picture. We were playing one night at the Beacon Theatre, and someone from my management company said they had someone they wanted me to talk to. It was Clive Davis. He was starting Arista, and he was looking for people who had songs and had production experience; since he was starting out from a flat start, he didn't have

producers or A&R people over there yet. So we had been working on a new album, what turned out to be [1975's] *The First Minute of a New Day*, and we named it that because Clive was having the first minute of a new day. He didn't like the picture of the gorilla sitting on the front, but it was done in his name.

It sounds like he treated you guys pretty well, and he really pushed the "Black Bob Dylan" angle.
Now, I didn't know about Bob Dylan. I had heard a few songs he had written, "Just Like a Woman" and "Like a Rolling Stone," and I liked both of those. But as far as him being something special that people wanted to be like, I'd never heard of him in that context. Clive said that so people could relate to what we did. But he never said that to me. As far as I knew, Dylan played harmonica, and I played piano. Dylan couldn't sing, and I could; that made us different right there.

You're finishing up a book called *Last Holiday* about Stevie Wonder's work to get Martin Luther King's birthday declared a national holiday. How important do you think Stevie's tour was to making that holiday a reality?
I think it brought a lot of attention to it. It was Stevie's tour and his campaign, and he allowed me to participate, and I was glad to do it. If you want to change America, you have to change the law. That's the only way to do it. You can burn down a lot of shit. You can tear down a lot of shit. You can go crazy and riot or whatever you want to do. Until you change the law, you haven't really changed the country. Stevie Wonder wanted to change the law to make it a national holiday, and that's what happened. I don't feel Stevie has received enough credit.

Do you feel that people get mixed up, especially when it comes to your lyrics, and confuse the difference between educating and being political, or educating versus inciting?
I don't believe that everyone understands that everything they do is more or less political. Because almost everything they touch has to do with taxes, and taxes sponsor their political society.

Are you very anti tax?
No, I just feel that I pay taxes, so I have a right to say where they're spent. I'd rather not see them spent killing people, that's all. I'm not against soldiers. I'm against war. I'd rather have money spent to do good. I'd rather Americans have the right to say where their tax money is spent. I'd like to see more spent on education.

I heard Kareem Abdul-Jabbar was your best man. Is that true?
Yeah, he introduced me to my wife. He lived in Dyckman House in New York, and we used to play ball together. When he went to UCLA, one of his classmates was the lady I ended up marrying. We used to play at the projects over there.

How did you do against Kareem?
Same way anybody else would have done. I was six foot three. When we started the band, he used to come over to the Roxy and sit in on percussion. Evidently, he played an album of ours that [my ex-wife] Brenda [Sykes] heard at his house, and she said she wanted to meet me. That's how I met her, and when we got married, he was our best man. We got married at Wayne Shorter's house, the guy in Weather Report. That was a great night. Kareem had to leave early because he was in training, left at eleven o'clock. But things went off without a hitch.

On the new album, *I'm New Here*, you sample Kanye West on "On Coming from a Broken Home." Did it feel good to sample someone else instead of getting sampled?
Not particularly. I worked with Malcolm Cecil, and he invented all those instruments that sampled things. Richard [Russell] thought that was comic. He sampled us, we sampled him. I thought it was funny.

Your track "Message to the Messengers," from 1994's *Spirits*, addressed rappers, telling them to be responsible. How do you feel your relationship has changed with them and with hip-hop?
I don't know. I haven't seen hip-hop lately. I see rappers as individuals. I know Mos Def. He's a good dude. We played Carnegie Hall together. Common, Kanye West, and those fellas, they're doing a great job. They're popular independently. You can't review someone's career when they're twenty-five. They're just getting on their feet. But I think they're going to be all right.

I remember talking with someone in the Last Poets, and he said when he was starting, the idea was to get more people to express themselves. Now that you look at the world that is hip-hop, do you feel responsible and happy that there are more people expressing themselves?
Yeah, I'm happy, but I wish they would express themselves instead of expressing something about the last rapper they heard. ○

Patrick Sisson is a Chicago-based writer and editor who wishes he could see Fred Anderson perform again.

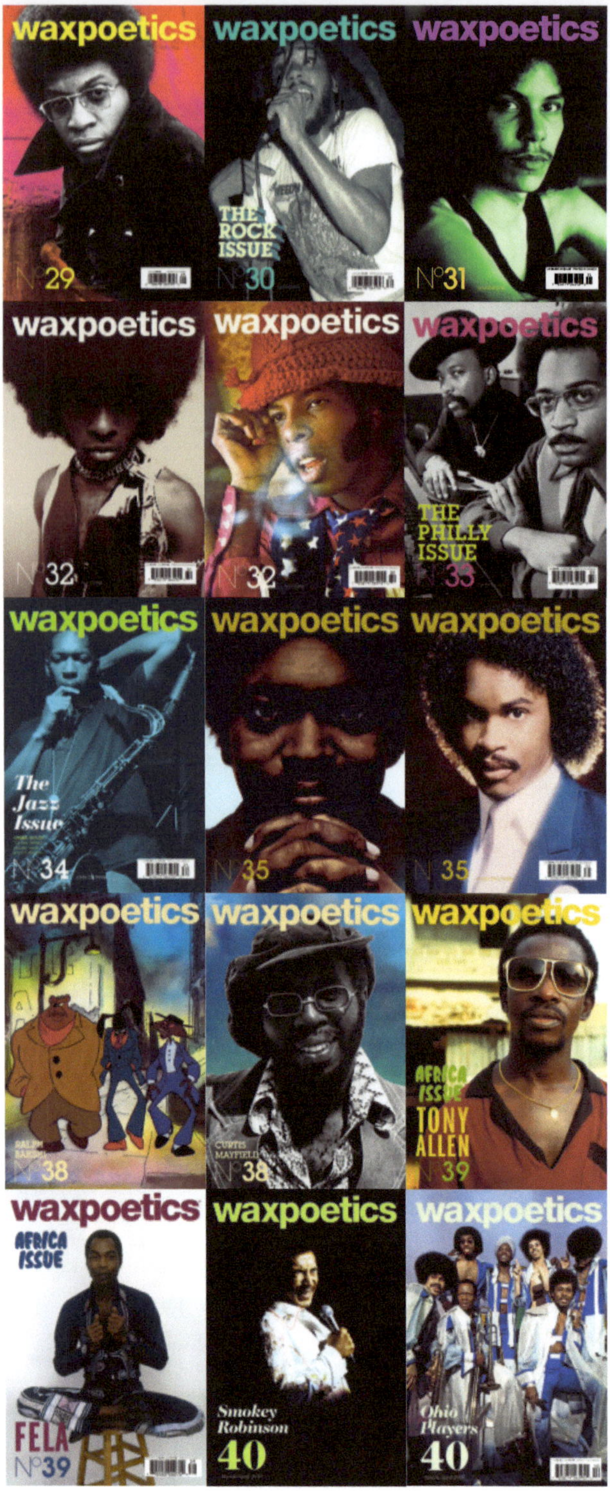

waxpoeticsbundles

PURCHASE ALL AVAILABLE BACK ISSUES AT A DISCOUNTED RATE AND RECEIVE FREE SHIPPING!

SAVE UP TO $100!

waxpoetics.com/storefront

Premium Subscriptions

- Same price as the newsstand
- Shipped quickly via USPS First Class Mail
- Protected in a secure cardboard mailer
- Upgrades available for current subscribers

waxpoetics.com/subscribe

Service for U.S. customers only. For subscription questions, email subscribe@waxpoetics.com

BIG LOVE

Barry White's unlimited passion took him to the heights of music

by **Michael A. Gonzales**

Photo by Laurens Van Houten/Frank White Photo Agency.

Barry White with his group Love Unlimited, including his second wife, Glodean (middle). Photo courtesy of Pictorial Press/Cache Agency.

Prelude to Seduction

It was winter of 1994, and I had just scored a sweet assignment to interview the king of "champagne soul," Barry White, in Europe. Arriving at the chaotic passport office the following morning, the middle-aged woman behind the counter popped her sweet, sticky gum and smirked. "So, why do you need to get your passport so fast?" she inquired sassily.

Smiling, I replied, "Because I'm going to Belgium to interview Barry White." Glancing at me as though she were hearing things, the snippy civil servant suddenly stopped smacking and simply stared. "Are you for real?" she stuttered. When I nodded my head, her smile was bright. "Come back after three o'clock, and it will be ready."

Indeed, Barry White has had that effect on women since speaking (not even singing) his steamy lines on Love Unlimited's "Walkin' in the Rain with the One I Love" in 1972. A household name for folks who grew up under the spell of stereophonic strings swelling from the soul kitchen back in the '70s, fans of kitschy pop culture, and crate diggers enticed by the constant samples, Barry White's sweet sounds have aged gracefully. A musical signifier for yearning, lust, and love in countless movies, television shows, various commercials, the smoothed-out tribute song "Love Unlimited" by Fun Lovin' Criminals, and Bill Cosby's still-hilarious 1976 parody "Yes, Yes, Yes," White's style is eternal.

"Producers had used strings in soul music before, but not the way Barry did," says manager and old friend Ned Shankman. "He played these big string sections like it was an individual artist. He had a brand-new sound that was so intoxicating." Shankman and White had been in business since the day Barry walked into his law office in 1972 looking for representation. "Barry had all the talent and intelligence, but he was pulling himself out of the ghetto," Shankman recalls. Barry, who was raising four children with his first wife, Betty, whom he had lost his virginity to in Exposition Park when he was fourteen, often hitchhiked into Hollywood looking for studio work. "He had holes in his shoes the size of silver dollars."

With gonzo rock critic Lester Bangs describing him as a "molasses-voiced monument," White reluctantly released his first single "I'm Gonna Love You Just a Little More, Baby" in 1973. Although White sang in a few doo-wop groups in the '60s and played drums for Jackie Lee on the road, after working as a producer, arranger, and A&R man, he preferred being behind the scenes.

"I like to be in the background," Barry said later. "Plus, I don't have a lot of respect for artists, because they want to be babysat. They want to call you at four in the morning, and if they don't have certain things in their dressing room, they [say] they're not going on. Most artists are babies, and I never wanted to be part of that."

Signed to 20th Century Records as a solo artist in 1972, seemingly overnight the former Watts street gang member transformed himself into one of the most popular performers on the planet. Joining forces with the late orchestrator/string arranger Gene Page—who that same year had done the *Blacula* soundtrack as well as fine-tuning White's "soft-porn, aural-chocolate sound," as critic Barney Hoskyns described it—White released successive gold and platinum albums over the next seven years.

Page, along with drummer Earl Palmer and saxophonist Plas Johnson, was one of the few Blacks down with the California posse of musicians later known as the Wrecking Crew. The collective played with producers Brian Wilson, Quincy Jones, Phil Spector, and Bones Howe, among others.

White and Page met in 1963 when they were paired as co-arrangers on Bob & Earl's addictive Marc Records single "Harlem Shuffle," a song the Rolling Stones remade in 1986. In the '60s, when White worked for Bob Keane's labels Del-Fi, Mustang, and Bronco, he hired Gene Page to do arrangements. During that same period, Page was recruited by Phil Spector to arrange strings for the Righteous Brothers' "You've Lost That Lovin' Feelin'" in 1964; he also worked with producer Lou Adler on "California Dreamin'" in 1965.

With a name that became synonymous with romance, Barry White's music was the aural equivalent of wine and roses, Jacuzzis and satin slippers. Combining simplistic soul grooves with lush arrangements, White created his own version of the California-soul style as popularized by Dionne Warwick and the 5th Dimension. Like the cool jazz of West Coast players Chet Baker, Art Pepper, and Gerry Mulligan, this was cool soul created by artists who were as at home with symphonic music as they were with R&B.

Influenced by the walls of sound Phil Spector constructed before losing his mind, the classical records his mom played in their Watts home, and the beauty of Holland-Dozier-Holland's many Motown jams, White's version of pop was bigger, Blacker, and sexier than anything that had come before it.

White's hits include "Never, Never Gonna Give Ya Up," "Can't Get Enough of Your Love, Babe," "You're the First, the Last, My Everything," and "Your Sweetness Is My Weakness." In 1974, he did the soundtrack for the underrated blaxploitation feature *Together Brothers*, which was funkier than his usual albums. Still, he didn't seem to think highly of the film. "I'm

not interested in police chases and guys selling dope on the corner," he said. "The only reason I did *Together Brothers* was because 20th Century led me to believe the movie was important to them, but it really wasn't. The movie didn't do nothing, but the album went platinum."

In addition to his own material, White penned and produced hits for offshoot groups Love Unlimited and the Love Unlimited Orchestra. He also produced various artists signed to his Soul Unlimited Productions including the following albums, mostly from 1974: Tom Brock's *I Love You More and More* (20th Century), Jay Dee's *Come on in Love* (Warner Bros.), Gene Page's *Hot City* (Atlantic), Gloria Scott's *What Am I Gonna Do?* (Casablanca), and White Heat's 1975 self-titled debut (RCA).

"None of those acts made any hits," says former White Heat member Greg Williams, who later cofounded the romantic Motown group Switch alongside keyboardist/vocalist Bobby DeBarge. Via telephone from his home in Los Angeles, Williams chuckles, "I can still see Barry now, walking into the studio wearing Bermuda shorts with his ashy legs."

Writing about White and Page's masterful "Love's Theme," which became the Love Unlimited Orchestra's signature song, author Alice Echols notes in *Hot Stuff: Disco and the Remaking of American Culture* (Norton, 2010), "White's single was remarkable for the way it upended the conventional wisdom about the marketing of music, and, like his recent R&B hits, it also underscored a trend in soul music away from the gritty and the raw."

After years of struggling, Barry White began creating the perfect '70s soundtracks for assimilation into the mainstream. This was the post-protest music for a new generation of Black folks who didn't demand the death of whitey, but instead Hustled with his women on integrated dance floors.

In fact, though Barry White hated being labeled a disco artist, his soul symphonies were the strobe-light highlight of any club night in the '70s. "What made Barry White the perfect Hustle music was that it wasn't too fast," says New York City teacher and Hustle champion Bryan Scott, who once danced to White's music at Leviticus. "Though a lot of dancers liked 'Love's Theme' best, my favorite was 'You're the First, the Last, My Everything.' Although the song still had a pulsating beat, there is still a coolness to it."

However, by the late '70s, Black music was going through a technical transformation, and, for he and his contemporaries Isaac Hayes and Curtis Mayfield, the reign of seasoned soul men soon ended. Although White signed a multimillion-dollar deal with CBS Records in 1979, releasing the ill-fated album *The Message Is Love*, the hits simply stopped coming, and it appeared that the maestro had lost his mojo.

In a crazy year that included the suicide of Donny Hathaway, rap music bubbling to the surface in the Bronx, Rod Stewart screeching about being sexy, and newcomers Shalamar zooming up the charts, the sound of young America was once again changing. Certainly, the same was true on the rock side, where surf music had evaporated and Hotel California had burned to the ground.

Yet, being a scamp from the time he was a boy, Barry White refused to stay down. Taking a hiatus from the business for a few years, he traveled around the world and worked in his RISE (Research in Sound Excellence) studio with musical director Jack Perry.

"Barry and I first met in 1969," Perry told me in 1994 as we stood backstage at the Vorst Nationaal, the venue where White was to perform. "He borrowed a Roberts reel-to-reel two-track to record the demo for Love Unlimited's 'Walkin' in the Rain with the One I Love,' and I didn't see him again until 1980."

Perry helped Barry build RISE, where the first album he recorded was a duet disc with his second wife and former Love Unlimited singer Glodean James. The studio was built in a separate house across from his residence and became Barry's home away from home from 1981 until 1993, when it was destroyed by an earthquake. One of the last songs recorded there before the earthquake was his 1994 comeback song, "Practice What You Preach."

Signing with A&M Records in 1987, he released *The Right Night & Barry White*, which contained the single "Sho' You Right." Still, it wasn't until three years later when White's old friend Quincy Jones recruited him to be part of a quartet that included El DeBarge, James Ingram, and Al B. Sure to sing on the stellar ballad "The Secret Garden (Sweet Seduction Suite)" that a real comeback effort was launched. As far as soul fans were concerned, that was when it became obvious that big daddy wasn't about to be ignored.

During this same period, Barry White began slipping back into our consciousness with television appearances, including a bugged episode of *The Simpsons* from 1993 called "Whacking Day." It wasn't the first time White had been animated, having appeared in Ralph Bakshi's controversial classic *Coonskin* (1975) as country-ass Sampson/Brother Bear.

Although White was a self-proclaimed "movie freak," with beautiful customized screening rooms in his mansion as well as RISE studio, he vowed never to make another film after *Coonskin*. "Bakshi is an animation genius, the way he mixed real life with the animation," White said. "I really respect him, but I didn't like being waken up at three in the morning to shoot something at one in the afternoon. Oliver Stone wanted to cast me in *The Doors* movie, but I told him, 'I'm a music person. Give that part to somebody striving to be an actor.'"

Not above making fun of his lover-man persona, Barry made a few guest appearances on the *Late Night with David Letterman* TV show, the funniest being an entire episode titled "Camping with Barry White" in 1983. When Letterman finally interviewed burly Barry, he admitted that his wife Glodean introduced him to the great outdoors. "Where I come from," White said, referring to the tough South Central, Los Angeles, neighborhood, "we camped on your chest or your doorstep." Although White was smiling, it was also his way of showing the world the badass behind the velvet jacket.

By the time I soared across the ocean and met the man who taught a generation of men how to talk shit but take it slow below the waist, Barry White achieved a Black pop coup by staging a comeback with his 1994 hit on A&M Records "Practice What You Preach," which was cowritten by Gerald Levert, who had had success beginning in the '80s with the R&B group Levert and whose father, Eddie, is a founding member of the O'Jays. Six years before our meeting inside his Four Seasons suite in Philadelphia, I'd seen the Jheri-curled Levert trio (featuring little brother Sean Levert and Marc Gordon) opening a sold-out Bobby Brown concert, new-jack swinging and singing their hits "Casanova" and "Just Coolin'" on the stage of Madison Square Garden.

"You wouldn't believe how many people in the music business dogged me when I said I had written songs for Barry White," Levert said. "'Why you want to give them tracks to Barry?' they said. 'He's old!' We forget that performers like Barry White have given us real music."

Watts Side Story

Growing up a child of television, I viewed Los Angeles as a mythical city controlled by Disney and sunshine: a place where everything was perfect and problems were solved by understanding sitcom parents like the Bradys, or Bill Bixby on *The Courtship of Eddie's Father* teaching his son life lessons as Harry Nilsson sang "Best Friend" in the background.

"Life is good in Los Angeles," says the voice of gossip junkie Sid Hudgens (Danny DeVito) in the beginning of *L.A. Confidential*. "It's paradise on earth." Yet, it wasn't until *Sanford and Son* premiered on NBC in 1972, the same year Love Unlimited released their debut single "Walkin' in the Rain with the One I Love," that pop culture began embracing the community known as Watts.

"Flat and impoverished, it is the last place on earth to look for the extraordinary or shadows of greatness," an announcer states about the community in a 1954 documentary on the bizarre Watts Towers. A shadow city within a city that most Caucasians simply ignored, Watts had its own music scene that had little impact on pop overall until rap exploded in the 1980s.

With artifacts like Charles Burnett's brilliant film *Killer of Sheep* in 1977, NWA's debut album in 1987, Walter Mosley's Bill Clinton–endorsed book *Devil in a Blue Dress* in 1990, and footage from the Rodney King uprising in 1992, America's various glimpses of the South Central community is usually soaked in blood.

Like many of the Black folks who flocked to Watts in the 1940s, Sadie Marie Carter migrated west from her home in Galveston, Texas, to the angelic lights of Los Angeles in search of something better. Yet, when young Miss Carter got pregnant by a married man, she returned briefly to her native city, to the loving arms of her sisters.

The city is known for being devastated by a hurricane in 1900, as well as the birthplace of legendary boxer Jack Johnson, who was known as the "Galveston Giant," and it was here on September 12, 1944, that Sadie gave birth to a baby boy she named Barrence Eugene Carter. Years later, back in Watts, when his daddy Melvin White was taking him to school, he crossed out Carter on the boy's birth certificate and inserted his own surname.

"It was that beautiful Taurus queen who made me interested in music," Barry told me about his mother in 1994, a month after his fiftieth birthday. "It's because of her I know music so well. Nobody's mother had a record collection like hers; she had stacks of 78s and knew every song on the radio, pop or Black. When I was four, she taught me how to harmonize, and the next year, saving fifty dollars from her welfare checks, she bought a good upright piano. That was when I started plucking around."

Clad in a black silk suit with no tie, big-boned Barry sat upright in a heavy oak chair inside a private tearoom at the Stanhope Hotel in Brussels. It was a few hours before showtime, when he, musical director Jack Perry, and a full orchestra would go onstage in front of the thousands packed inside the Vorst Nationaal theater.

Yet, instead of resting up before the two-hour show, White cheerfully rode the Pacific Electric Railway down memory lane, back to the house on Fourteenth and Paloma he shared with his mother, little brother Darryl (who was thirteen months his junior), and that first piano in the living room. "My mother

silence. Without a doubt, it couldn't have been easy for a young boy growing up in Watts to admit to his street-corner homeboys that he enjoyed doing something that could be considered sissified.

As Thomas Pynchon once noted in an essay about Watts, "Violence is never far from you." While the bang-bang boogie of the Bloods and Crips has had better marketing, including the countless platinum soundtracks fueled by Dr. Dre, Eazy-E, Ice Cube, Snoop Dogg, and Tupac, many folks aren't aware that even back in the 1950s, South Central gangs were banging.

Years before flicks like *Boyz n the Hood*, *South Central*, or *Menace II Society* celebrated the cinematic charisma of California wild boys, gangs with names like the Gladiators and the Slausons were doing their thing in the '50s and '60s. Said Barry, "Southwest Los Angeles had four or five gangs; Westside had eleven or twelve gangs. The first gang I was in was called the Roaming Twenties, and then I joined the hottest gang around, the Businessmen.

"People don't understand young people's frustration," Barry continued. "The greatest thing ever to happen to young people today is rap music, because it's an outlet for that frustration. It gets it out of them."

Sharing a tight bond with his brother, Darryl, who ran alongside Barry and the local hoods, Barry and his brother couldn't afford to buy the club jacket that featured a muscular devil with wings and the name "Businessmen" underneath. "One night, we had a meeting, and there was, like, three hundred guys there," said White. "And I told everybody, the more we wear these jackets, the more the police know right where we are. Most stopped wearing them that night.

"We was the Businessmen, which meant we was in the business of taking care of business," White bragged. For the first time, I realized that his famous rap-style singing voice has its origins in the poetic parlance of smooth-tongued hoods on Central Avenue shooting dice, playing pool, and talking smack.

"My mother wanted us to quit," Barry said. "She was convinced that we was going to kill somebody or somebody was going to kill us. One day, I got pissed and screamed, 'How you think you walking up and down these streets at night? How you think you able to do that without getting robbed?' I told her we went to dances and sometimes fought, but I didn't tell her the crime shit."

Of course, it was only a matter of time before Sadie realized her sons were far from saints when baby brother Darryl got popped for the first time when he was eight years old. "He was the one who taught me how to fight," Barry recalled.

"We'd be somewhere, and he always liked to fight. His idea of harmony was confusion, people screaming and hollering; he loved that shit. He told me, 'Once they see you're a fighter, you don't have to worry about getting jumped.' I'd seen guys get arrested before, but they were wimps. Soon as the police came after them, they'd go into hiding and crying and all that shit. My brother never did that. He'd wait for the cops to come get him.

"During the Watts riots, my mother kept saying, 'I'm so glad your brother's in jail, I don't know what to do.' Darryl was as committed to crime as much as I was to music." Released from Folsom Prison (made famous by Johnny Cash's live album) in 1977, Darryl was murdered six years later. He was thirty-eight.

Still, when Barry was a teenager, he had his own crime spree going down in the streets of Watts. "For about eleven months, I couldn't go to sleep without stealing a car," remembered White. "I must've stolen about hundred and fifty, two hundred cars." However, it wasn't until Barry White got his own taste of life behind bars for stealing a bunch of tires that he figured he'd better "straighten up and fly right," as Capitol Records star Nat King Cole used to sing. After seven months inside, White was released on August 28, 1960. "I made a vow that I wasn't going back to jail ever again," Barry remembered. He was sixteen years old.

Walls of Soul

While Los Angeles is often referred to as a studio town when talking about movie companies, the term could also be applied to the many recording studios scattered throughout the city beginning in the 1950s. From Sinatra over at Capitol to Phil Spector slaving at Gold Star to the doo-wop soul boys in South Central to the first waves of surf music taped in suburban garages, there was no shortage of spaces to create new pop anthems for the world to devour.

Three days after being released from prison, Barry found himself inside TGG Studios over on Highland Boulevard meeting postal worker/record executive Lummie Fuller. Forming Lummtone Records in 1959, Fuller recorded thirty-six songs on eighteen sides through 1965. Recording mostly doo-wop, groups signed to Lummtone included the Colognes, the Elgins, George Powell and the Troopers, the Five Ramblers, and the group White was auditioning for, the Upfronts.

"In those days, you could record a hot record on Tuesday night and have it on streets and on radio by Wednesday,"

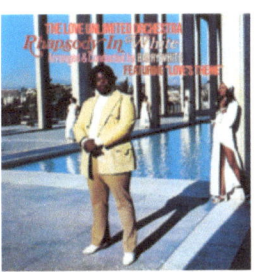

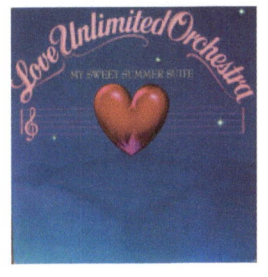
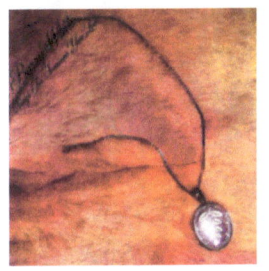

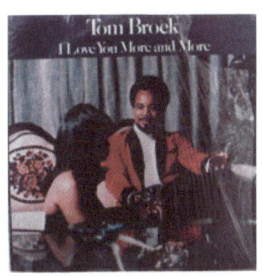

Shankman says. While excited to be chosen, the teenage White's real highlight was discovering the magic kingdom of sound contained within the small music factory: "When I walked into that room where that big mixing board was with those knobs and big-ass meters and the tape recorder, I just stood against the wall and observed everything in that room. I knew that was where I wanted to be."

For the next nine years, White put in work at various studios, played drums on the road for Jackie Lee, and was doing what he needed to do to stay in the business. Although his homey Gene Page would pass him loot whenever he could, Barry's Businessmen pride was getting the best of him. While he had his first wife and their four kids at home, he was still sleeping on recording-room floors instead of going home.

However, in 1970, when White first met the fine foxes who'd eventually become his first mega-success, Love Unlimited, he knew that Diane Taylor and sisters Linda and Glodean James could be his Supremes, his Ronettes, his ticket out of Watts forever.

"I met them at a friend's recording studio," Barry said. "They were a strange blend, because they had heavy voices. Like, Toni Braxton heavy, Anita Baker heavy. Love Unlimited was the first complete album [1972's *From a Girl's Point of View We Give You...*] I had ever done. I went underground for seven months. I would write from morning to morning. I'd close my eyes for a minute on the couch, and then it was back to the music. From that, I got my first million seller with 'Walkin' in the Rain.'"

Prior to working on the Love Unlimited album, Gene Page snuck Barry into a closed Holland-Dozier-Holland session so the young producer could observe his aural idols at work. "Gene lied and said I was a backup singer," White said, laughing. "Holland-Dozier-Holland showed Black men and women that it ain't just about bass, drum, and guitar. They wrote songs that took my head in another direction of music. Those guys were my deans."

In the same way that a blaxploitation character ain't jack without a dope theme song, great pop auteurs can't compete without their own studio. So, in the same way Phil Spector had taken over Gold Star in the '60s, White made Whitney Studios in Glendale his headquarters throughout the '70s. "I found Whitney, because I wanted a studio that wasn't in Hollywood," White confessed. "I wanted to be in private and serenity and peace when I cut that Love Unlimited album. The only other people who cut there were Hanna-Barbera's cartoon overdubs and choirs recording Christmas albums. After I cut Love Unlimited, then I did my solo record there. Wasn't nobody from the hip side of the business recording there, but when I opened it up and blew it up, they started coming."

Greg Williams, whose band White Heat was signed to Soul Unlimited Productions and also played at White and Glodean's wedding in 1973, says, "Barry loved the sound at Whitney Studios." Having sat in on the Whitney studio sessions in 1973 for *Can't Get Enough*, Williams reveals, "Barry always started with the drums, that was his foundation, because they held the groove; then the melody, then the lush string arrangements. He'd tell Page how he wanted the violins on top of the cello. He'd scream, 'Make the motherfuckers dance, Gene!' I learned a lot from Barry about arranging; he'd tell me about when he was a drummer, and I loved the way he would direct Gene on the strings. Not taking anything away from Gene, because he was a genius," Williams continues, "but Barry had very definite ideas about what he wanted."

Although White relied on Gene Page to write the charts, White communicated with the band musically by "humming it to them or playing the line on a piano." He adds, "Like I told my mother, to know music isn't to write it or read it, it's about feeling it." And, for the next ten years, Whitney was where Barry White *felt* it.

In 1999, Barry White released his last disc, *Staying Power*, which included duets with Chaka Khan and Lisa Stansfield; the album went on win two Grammy Awards. Four years later, on July 4, 2003, White died at Cedars-Sinai Medical Center in Los Angeles. He was fifty-eight.

Seeing pictures in *Jet* magazine of his cremation ashes scattered from a yacht off the California coast, I thought about Barry telling me, "Music is sacred always. Music is the most powerful element to human peace, tranquility, heartaches, and heartbreaks. Music has something in it that if you're up, it can take you higher, and if you're down, it can take you lower.

"Shit, did she walk out on you? Took all the furniture and left you the toilet paper sitting in the middle of the floor? Get your favorite tune and play that son of a bitch. It will take you down lower than where you are. And through that same song, it'll bring you back up." Sho' you right. ○

Michael A. Gonzales writes about pop culture for various magazines. He is the senior writer for Soulsummer.com and lives in Brooklyn. Barney Hoskyns's brilliant *Waiting for the Sun: Strange Days, Weird Scenes, and the Sound of Los Angeles* (St. Martin's Press, 1996) was an invaluable resource while writing this story.

Tru Thoughts recordings

Distributed in the USA by EMI

 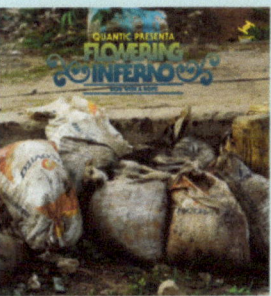  

Various
OUT NOW
Tru Thoughts Funk
Essential Tru Thoughts compilation showcasing some of the most acclaimed, incendiary funk music of our era from The Bamboos, The Quantic Soul Orchestra, Alice Russell, Hot 8 Brass Band and more.

Quantic Presenta Flowering Inferno
July 13th
Dog With A Rope
Quantic brings a tropical soundclash of dub and reggae flavours to the Latin American and African sounds that he has been chasing round the globe since he first started collecting records.

Saravah Soul
July 27th
Cultura Impura
Second album from the half Brazilian, half British, London based purveyors of Afro-meets Brazilian funk. This vibrant record sees the band channelling '60s Brazil via 21st Century East London.

Various
September 14th
Tru Thoughts Compilation
An essential collection highlighting some of the amazing music from Tru Thoughts. Including Quantic, Bonobo, Alice Russell, Belleruche, Beth Rowley and Stonephace feat Adrian Utley (Portishead).
All for under $5

Visit www.tru-thoughts.co.uk for all tour dates, releases & news.
All Tru Thoughts & Unfold music is available direct from www.etchshop.co.uk, or from Amazon & iTunes

---

[W]hat makes **Post-Nothing** such a thrill is the manner in which **Japandroids** hold absolutely nothing back. As contagious as any of the lyrics, melodies, riffs, or drum fills are, their energy and lack of self-consciousness is every bit as equally lovable.
Pitchfork / Best New Music 8.3

Chord by chord, '90s distortion seems to be oozing back into guitar rock. And for those jonesing for that sort of tar and fuzz, Vancouver's **Japandroids** come bearing gifts.
Onion A.V. Club / "A"

Critically acclaimed album made over thirty year-end lists including *The Onion*, *NME*, *Spin*, *Stereogum*, and *Chicago Tribune*.

Take 15% off your next Polyvinyl E-Store order with coupon code: **WAXPOETICS**

www.polyvinylrecords.com | info@polyvinylrecords.com

In the Raw

D'Angelo's organic sweet soul shook up modern R&B

by **Michael A. Gonzales**

Singer, songwriter, and musician Michael Eugene Archer, who later adopted the jiggy stage name D'Angelo, released his groundbreaking album, *Brown Sugar*, in 1995. Though only twenty-one, he changed the sound of R&B, creating an entirely new genre called neo-soul. In the same way Ray Charles master-mixed juke-joint vibes and Sunday-morning gospel, baby-faced D'Angelo created an intoxicating fusion of Southern soul and East Coast hip-hop that transcended the R&B genre.

As a stirring cycle of songs ripe with raw romanticism, funky sensuality, haunting lyricism, dirty grooves, and laid-back attitude, *Brown Sugar* was arguably the last great soul album of the millennium. Blending Southern vocal phrasings with big-city cool, D'Angelo's music possessed a similar rhythmic spirit as his yesteryear FM radio heroes who once made records for Stax, Motown, and Atlantic.

Recorded from 1993 to 1995, D'Angelo utilized the talents of producers (and later friends) Raphael Saadiq, Ali Shaheed Muhammad, and Bob Power to create a stellar collection of soul songs that were instant classics. "My music is left of mainstream, but not too abstract," D'Angelo told *Billboard* three months before *Brown Sugar*'s release.

First migrating to bustling New York City in the early 1990s, D'Angelo was a sensitive, down-home kid from Richmond, Virginia. Mumbling between drags on a constant Newport cigarette, he often avoided eye contact and hid behind a self-constructed wall that protected his fragility from the world.

"D'Angelo was just a shy, humble guy when we met," says Tribe Called Quest member and producer Ali Shaheed Muhammad, who produced the title track. "He was just a regular dude who loved music."

Yet, somewhere between *Brown Sugar* and sophomore gem *Voodoo*, released five years later, D'Angelo became a reckless rock star, and his crash back to Earth was inevitable.

After a staggering Fitzgerald-esque crack-up during the Voodoo Tour in 2000, D'Angelo retreated from the limelight, and his problems with depression, drugs, and drink became public knowledge.

In 2002, he was pepper-sprayed and arrested in his hometown of Richmond, Virginia. Three years later, he was picked up on drunk-driving and drug charges. More importantly for the cult of D'Angelo, his inability to finish a long-awaited third album became legendary.

"I don't want people telling me how great I sound, and then I don't build on that sound," D'Angelo told me in 1995. Hired by EMI publicist Karen Taylor to write D'Angelo's record company bio, I met D'Angelo for brunch at the Chelsea eatery Viceroy Café a few months before *Brown Sugar* was released on July 3. "What I make next week should sound better than what I did today."

Born February 11, 1974, D'Angelo was only a baby when Curtis Mayfield, Al Green, and Sly Stone blared from radios across America's chocolate cities. Still, when growing up, he valued those musical giants and dug deep within those funky influences while finishing his debut.

"What made *Brown Sugar* so unconventional was that D'Angelo combined Southern church music on top of jazzy hip-hop," explains Gary Harris, the former EMI Records A&R man who signed D'Angelo to the label in 1993. "In some circles, being Southern is stigmatized as country or unsophisticated. But clearly, D was more progressive, and his sound just took off."

Encouraged by Harris to stay in Richmond until his demos were complete, D'Angelo wrote songs and developed the *Brown Sugar* sound in his bedroom. Recorded on a four-track and using a cheap microphone, D'Angelo had a plan. "I didn't want to overproduce the shit," D'Angelo said. "I wanted it to sound raw,

not real polished. Soul music is not limited, because there's so much blues and gospel in it. I tried to stay true to that."

Having completed demos for eight songs a few months later, D'Angelo moved to midtown Manhattan. Staying at the Penta Hotel across the street from Madison Square Garden, he later relocated to the infamous Chelsea Hotel. Although he didn't like New York City in the beginning, D'Angelo soon learned to maneuver through the streets of the city without problem.

"I had a studio on Sixteenth Street and Union Square, and D would walk over there all the time from the Chelsea," remembers famed recording engineer and producer Bob Power fourteen years later.

Power, who has produced, engineered, and mixed albums for Erykah Badu, De La Soul, the Roots, and Macy Gray, also worked with the arty hip-hop group A Tribe Called Quest, whom D'Angelo was enamored with. It was Tribe member Ali Shaheed Muhammad who introduced D'Angelo to Power in 1993; that same year, Power also coproduced Me'Shell Ndegéocello's acclaimed debut, *Plantation Lullabies*.

"D was only nineteen years old when we first met, but his demos were fucking amazing," says Power. "The challenge of working on *Brown Sugar* was figuring out how to make the material into a record without losing the cool shit. If you really want to break it down, that was the balance on that record for me." Mixing six songs on *Brown Sugar*, Power also coproduced "Alright," "Me and Those Dreamin' Eyes of Mine," "Shit, Damn, Motherfucker," "Smooth," and "Higher." The two worked together both at Battery Studios (where A Tribe Called Quest also recorded) and inside Power's Union Square loft.

Power soon found himself waiting hours for D'Angelo to show up for sessions. "It took us six to eight months to complete six songs," Power remembers, "because D was just habitually late. I ended up walking off the project, because I just didn't have the time anymore. It was obvious he was more comfortable doing it alone."

Brown Sugar not only transformed R&B, it also changed the life of its creator. From preacher's kid to overnight sensation, D'Angelo was hyperbolically billed as "the son of soul" and greatness was expected.

Creating the *Brown Sugar* tracks with an Ensoniq EPS-16, a primitive sequencer and keyboard in one, D was able to mimic whatever instruments he wanted. Combining live instrumentation with hip-hop-production aesthetics, D'Angelo applied many memories of dusty grooves to create a hypnotic, hybrid sound.

"D'Angelo sang in between the chords, and on the backgrounds, he didn't sing the full chords," says Ali Shaheed Muhammad. "D has an interesting way of structuring melodies and phrasings, and all of his background vocals were really stacked. D might've been haunted by Marvin Gaye, but he was also a hip-hop head who grew up in the church. He had a lot of things going on inside his head."

Indeed, this was soul filtered through the ears of kids who grew up listening to the gritty soundscapes of rap producers Marley Marl and the Bomb Squad but had no problem digesting the old-school sounds of Curtis Mayfield, Willie Mitchell, Norman Whitfield, and Marvin Gaye.

"D was able to put music together like no one else," Power explains. "Vocally, he was the only one singing behind the beat at that time. It was often hard to understand what he was saying, but sometimes it sounded like D was singing in his own language."

Though the rough textures of the songs were smoothed out during the recording process, D originally wanted *Brown Sugar* to be gritty as *Voodoo* was five years later. In terms of the dirty style he initially wanted to hear on *Brown Sugar*, some fans believe D'Angelo compromised his sonic vision.

"I don't call it smoothed out," Power says. "I just helped him make a record the way I know how to make a quality record: warm, fat, and present." Nevertheless, compromised or not, *Brown Sugar* sounded like no other record on the market.

Although D'Angelo played most of the instruments himself, producer Bob Power added a little ax to the project. "On 'These Dreamin' Eyes of Mine,' I replayed one of D's keyboard solos on guitar, while on 'Alright,' I was doing some Wah Wah Watson shit," he says with a laugh. Still, when a friend at Blue Note Records suggested they use upright jazz bassist Larry Grenadier on "Smooth," Power wasn't sure how D might play alongside the new-jack jazzbo.

"He had played me the demos, and I thought the whole record was killing," Grenadier says. "D'Angelo's chops were so unique that whether he played soul or jazz, it just sounded like him. However, on 'Smooth,' he played this Basie-like minimalist thing that was perfect."

Staying at the studio for hours, Grenadier contributed bass on a few tracks, but only his work on "Smooth" made it to *Brown Sugar*. "Bob wanted that intro on the record," he says, "but the way D'Angelo plays, he really didn't need to have much more bass on there. To me, D's demos sounded pretty finished."

Befriending D'Angelo during the *Voodoo* sessions, Brooklyn singer Sun Singleton says, "People don't realize how well schooled D is in jazz. Really, he is a jazz dude. He'd be in the studio smoking some high-potent weed, and, next thing, he was at the piano improvising. It was so fascinating watching

his fingers slide across the keys."

On the walls of the midtown Manhattan offices of D'Angelo's first manager, Kedar Massenburg, hang platinum and gold plaques earned by D'Angelo as well as plaques earned by Massenburg's other discoveries: Erykah Badu, India.Arie, and Chico DeBarge. "I first met D'Angelo when I was working with Stetsasonic," Kedar explains. "He was trying to be a rapper at the time."

A few years later, the two were reintroduced by music publisher Jocelyn Cooper of Midnight Music, and Kedar signed him on as a client. "D'Angelo was doing soul music, but he didn't look like a soul artist," Kedar continues. "He wasn't wearing suits at the time, so we had to find a way to market him. We decided on that vintage look; even the album cover was an homage to *What's Going On*. There were no other artists like him at the time, and a lot of setup and strategy went into the *Brown Sugar* project."

As D'Angelo freely admitted, he admired the funky ideas of the '70s soul generation. "Marvin and the artists back then, they were setting trends. They were coming up with unique shit," D'Angelo proclaimed. "The state of R&B was in a rut [when I was making my album]. Everybody was so commercial, and nobody was trying to make real shit." Experimenting with various vintage instruments, old-fashioned microphones, and sometimes even analog recording methods, D'Angelo created the R&B subgenre soon to be called neo-soul. By 1995, the concept of neo-soul was sold to audiences who were already R&B fans but had grown tired of lame R&B.

"I always felt that the term neo-soul applied more to the making of music but not the sound," says India.Arie from her home in Atlanta. "We were just young Black artists looking for wider musical parameters to express ourselves. While I enjoyed D's second album, *Voodoo*, to me, it lacks the traditional song structure that is prevalent on *Brown Sugar*. From the singing to the playing to the production, *Brown Sugar* is a classic album."

Despite the fact that no emerging artists (Jill Scott, Bilal, Amy Winehouse) ever referred to their sound as neo-soul, the marketing phrase caught on with music journalists as well as the public. "Before the sound was called neo-anything, it was just D'Angelo's music," declares singer/songwriter Anthony Hamilton, who sang backup with D'Angelo on the Voodoo Tour. "*Brown Sugar* is a great album that is very critical to the history of soul music. All these years after its initial release, it's still an influence. After *Brown Sugar*, there was no turning back."

As one of the architects of the retro-soul sound before it was neo, multitalented singer/songwriter/producer Raphael Saadiq, formerly of Tony! Toni! Toné!, was brought in to toil with D'Angelo. Working on the West Coast, the collaboration produced what would become the seductive third single, "Lady." Although "Lady" was released after "Brown Sugar" and the Smokey Robinson cover "Cruisin'," it would be D'Angelo's first gold record.

"I wrote 'Lady' in a Marriott Hotel lobby in Connecticut," Raphael told me in a 2009 interview. "There was a piano sitting there, and I just sat down and started writing this song about a girl I knew who lived in Long Island. I originally played it for the members of Tony! Toni! Toné!, but they didn't like it. I remember them saying, 'Everything you write is not a hit.' So, I put it away.

"Four years later, D'Angelo ended up coming to my house. This lady who was our music publisher at the time introduced us, and he came over to [Pookie Lab] and heard the song. He said he liked it a lot, and we started working on it. When we worked, we just goofed around, ordered food, and played. It wasn't really work; it was more like playing a pickup game with your boy.

"I had my back turned to him when he started playing keyboards," Saadiq continued. "I just turned around and was like, 'Wow!' I was blown away. Later, I remember D'Angelo wanted to sing the backgrounds himself. At the time, the studio was in my garage in Sacramento, so I left; by the time I came back, I couldn't believe what he had done to the backgrounds. It was crazy how good it sounded."

In 1995, explaining how much Saadiq had to do with enriching his musical education, D'Angelo said, "Ray schooled me about the music business and music in general. I stayed at his house for four days when we recorded 'Lady,' fucking around with a lot of ideas and listening to a lot of music."

According to Raphael, years later while working on "Untitled (How Does It Feel)," the groundbreaking Prince homage from *Voodoo*, D'Angelo confessed that he hadn't really liked "Lady" much when they recorded it, because he thought it was too simple. Raphael adds, "D was trying to be very complex. But when people started telling him how they had made babies to that track, he appreciated it more."

Shortly after Raphael Saadiq finished working with D'Angelo, the dapper musician was in New York City chilling with homeboy Ali Shaheed Muhammad. Not only was the Tribe Called Quest beat-fiend good friends with Saadiq, but the two had collaborated on Tony! Toni! Toné!'s 1993 double-platinum disc, *Sons of Soul*; in 1999, he would join forces with Raphael and En Vogue singer Dawn Robinson for the acclaimed Lucy

Pearl project.

"I had known the Tonys' music since *The Revival* album, but it wasn't until we began recording together that we became close," Ali says from his home in New Jersey. "We had worked together at a studio in Trinidad, and he became like an older brother. To this day, I'm humbled when anyone wants to work with me, especially singers. So, when Raphael first called on me, I thought it was the strangest thing."

Formed in 1985, A Tribe Called Quest began their careers as part of the Native Tongues posse. Like contemporaries Prince Paul, Pete Rock, and DJ Premier, producer Ali Muhammad was unafraid to create jazzy, soulful turntable music that took the sound of hip-hop literally to the next level.

While Ali might be modest when describing his own talents behind the boards, as the cocreator of rhythmic hip-hop classics *People's Instinctive Travels and the Paths of Rhythm* (1990), *The Low End Theory* (1991), and *Midnight Marauders* (1993), he was a pioneer of infusing jazz, laid-back soul, and hip-hop that created a new flavor in rap music. "Before Tribe and Gang Starr, hip-hop was kind of stiff," Muhammad explains. "I don't mean stiff in a bad way, but the music we created just had a different kind of movement and flow to it. Be it the bass lines, chord structures, or the different time signatures, the music always moved."

Hyping D'Angelo's talents, Raphael played demo versions of "Lady" and "Alright" and told Ali that the soul boy wanted to work with him. "There was already so much depth and color in his work, I couldn't figure out why he felt he needed me. I was in shock."

Vibing together at his home studio in Jersey City, Ali and D'Angelo played around on a preproduction level. "It was cool, because we had sampled different things, got a couple of songs together, but they were just beats and loops," Ali says. "But the real work didn't happen until we started working at Studio C over at Battery." The "itty-bitty room" where Tribe often worked, Battery's Studio C wasn't the most high-tech spot in Manhattan, but it was a favorite of Ali's. "I worked a lot with computers in my music, but the computers in Studio C crashed so much, I began to joke that the room was haunted."

During one of the lulls when the engineer was trying to work through the bugs in the computer program, D'Angelo sat at the piano and just started playing. "At first, it sounded like intermission music," says Ali. "But then he started playing this chord progression, and I stopped and looked at him. Even he wasn't aware of what exactly he was playing, he just had his hands on the keyboard. When I asked him what he was playing, he said, 'Nothing.'"

Having gotten used to keeping a DAT steadily taping during his sessions ("you never know what you might pick up"), Ali heard something in the "nothing" D'Angelo was playing. "I spent ten minutes tracking what was on my computer and instantly called up a new song," Ali explains. After taking two minutes to program a beat, Ali told D, " 'Play that thing on top that you were playing before.' Afterwards, we sat and stared at each other, and D'Angelo just started laughing, because he knew what I knew.

"Next thing, D played bass on top of those chords and went over it with some lines. He said, 'Hold up. Can we sit with this for a second?' Maybe another fifteen minutes went by before he finally went into the booth and started doing the backgrounds, and that's how the title track, 'Brown Sugar,' came to be. It was like it was too good to be true, because that song came out of twenty minutes and a mistake."

Although "Brown Sugar" was D'Angelo's debut single as well as the only track on the album nominated for a Grammy, the label at first wasn't pleased with the final result. "You have to realize, at the time, nothing else had that sound," says Ali. "EMI kept insisting that the song was too raw and needed to be finished. I admired the brains and musical knowledge of Gary Harris, but he was another one who kept saying he didn't think that 'Brown Sugar' was finished. It was cool that we were later nominated for the Grammy, but what is cooler to me is the fact that 'Brown Sugar' was the spawn of a new movement. That song has a different texture and feel than everything else on that album."

Although they continued to collaborate in New York and later at Raphael's space in Sacramento, where the trio considered starting a super soul group called Lynwood Rose, no other D'Angelo/Ali tracks were ever released.

"Unless I had supernatural powers, it would've been impossible for me to predict that he would soon become a sex symbol, one of the most sought-after musicians in the world, and one of the greatest voices on the planet," says Ali. "I just feel blessed that we even had the opportunity to sit in the room together."

It was a drizzly gray Sunday afternoon in the spring of 1995 when I first met D'Angelo. Sporting tight cornrows, the twenty-one-year-old wore jeans and Timberlands. An unassuming cat, D'Angelo was a little pudgy and far from the chiseled Adonis he would become a few years later.

"What's up?" he greeted me, shaking my hand. D'Angelo talked in a molasses manner that made me believe he had never rushed to do anything. Standing at the tin bar, I pulled a pack of Newports from my pocket. "Can I bum one of your

Photo by Beth Herzhaft

cigarettes?" he asked. D'Angelo had a sleepy-eyed gaze that comes from too many blunts and late studio nights. Without hesitation, I handed him the cigarettes.

Having listened to the *Brown Sugar* advance about a hundred times prior to our meeting, I babbled about the jazzy textures on "When We Get By," the soulful "Me and Those Dreamin' Eyes of Mine," the silky vocals of the Smokey Robinson cover "Cruisin'," the boldness of the blues brooding of "Shit, Damn, Motherfucker," and the lush nickel-bag love of the title track.

"Most people who try to do something different don't get any recognition," D'Angelo observed. "But I knew when I came with my shit, I wasn't going to sound like anybody else."

The son of a Pentecostal preacher, Luther Archer Sr., D'Angelo was baptized Michael Eugene Archer. Messing about with the piano since he was a toddler, his favorite toys were the ebony and ivory keys. "When I first learned how to walk, I was banging on the piano," he reminisced. "My parents had bought one for my brother, but I would sit down and play songs that I had heard on the radio."

The first two songs Michael learned to play were Donna Summer's "Hot Stuff" and Earth, Wind & Fire's "Boogie Wonderland." Still, every Saturday afternoon, he was inside his daddy's house of worship, Refugee Temple Assembly of Yahweh Yahoshua the Messiah Church, learning new spirituals for Sunday morning. "My father played a lot of gospel songs by artists like Mahalia Jackson, Walter Hawkins, and Maggie Ingram," he said. "That was the kind of music I was around then."

Listening to "Higher," the last track on *Brown Sugar*, one can clearly hear D'Angelo's divine inspiration. "Please give us strength, Lord, to fight our battles / and we can walk on the streets of gold," he sings. "'Cause you take me higher, further than the sky above / send me in ecstasy, baby, with your love." With churchy harmonies, Hammond organ, and the subtle guitar of Bob Power, "Higher" sounded like D'Angelo making love in the amen corner.

"I wrote a lot of bullshit songs when I was little, but the first real song I ever wrote and performed was a gospel song," said D'Angelo. "I had my own choir at my father's church, and when I was sixteen, I wrote a song for us to sing. After that, I just started writing more and more."

Although D'Angelo played excellent piano by ear, he didn't receive formal lessons until he was twelve years old. "My teacher was the same strict nun who had taught my brother: Sister Wright," he explained. "She tried to teach me to read music, but I rejected her lessons. When she was trying to teach me how to read, I thought, 'I don't need that shit.' I wanted to play what I wanted to play."

Inspired by the grooves of a different keyboardist, D'Angelo began studying the work of "Prince, Prince, and Prince." At the age of twelve, the same year D'Angelo was beginning to master his instrument, Prince's 1986 hit "Kiss" was steadily climbing the charts. "Everything he did was the bomb," D'Angelo gushed. "And, he could do it all himself. I was one of those kids reading the album credits. I knew back then that I wanted to do that type of shit."

When I mentioned collecting Prince non-album B-sides, citing "She's Always in My Hair" as a favorite, D yelled, "That's my shit! That's my shit!" Interrupted by the waiter, who walked us over to the black leather booth, D'Angelo and I sat down. "I'm going to leave you guys," the publicist said. Minutes after she'd left, D and I ordered potent Long Island Iced Teas along with our meal.

Although D'Angelo rarely talked about his father, one might imagine that his old man wasn't completely thrilled with his youngest son admiring the sexy, secular sounds of the androgynous musician. "My parents split up when I was real young," D'Angelo confessed. "I lived with my mother." While his older brothers were away at school, D was dealing with the drama from a recently broken family. "My mother was going through a lot of shit being on her own," he explained. "She was exploring a new section of her life, and I was with her. We struggled, me and her, but we hung in there."

During that time, church was the extent of the relationship between D and his father. Nevertheless, as D got older, even that began to fade. "After a certain time, he left it up to us whether we wanted to go to church or not. Whatever we wanted to do with our lives, he kind of left that decision up to us."

During his mid-teens, D, like an entire generation of young Black boys coming of age at the height of America's crack epidemic, got caught up glorifying hood gangstars and getting into trouble with the law. "I got knocked off course for a minute. I got into a fight with a cop. Sitting in jail, I felt like I had come to the crossroads. I felt like God was talking to me."

When D'Angelo was sixteen, he formed a singing group with his cousins, calling themselves Michael Archer and Precise. The sharp-dressed crew sported high-top fades and genie pants while playing covers of Smokey Robinson's "Cruisin'," Entouch's "II Hype," and Soul II Soul's "Back to Life" at family reunions and talent shows.

"The only real scene in Richmond was the talent shows," D'Angelo said. "There were two dancers and four background singers. I sequenced the music, one cousin programmed it, and another cousin was on drums. We'd be wearing our Bobby Brown/MC Hammer gear, but we used to rock. Otherwise, there is no real outlet for young talent in Richmond. They closed most of the clubs because of shoot-outs, so ain't shit down there really."

Eventually, the group was spotted by a talent scout who offered them a slot on the amateur competition of *Showtime at the Apollo*. Kids who had never been far from home, Michael Archer and Precise made their big-city debut on the same stage where James Brown recorded his landmark live album in 1962.

"I had never been out of Richmond, so just coming to New York was wild," he muttered. "I was so excited to see 125th Street. But soon as the MC announced that I was from Richmond, the crowd started booing. I just closed my eyes and started singing that old Peabo Bryson song, 'Feel the Fire.' I wanted to get it over with, but I wasn't going to let them boo me off." Moments later, the same badly behaved folks were cheering. "We came in third place, but the next time we went, we came in first."

Yet just when it seemed that Michael Archer and Precise might be a success, D'Angelo decided to follow his own muse. "I didn't want to do the band thing anymore," he said, finishing his cocktail. "I just wanted to get my music moving. I wanted to get signed. I didn't know if it was going to happen when I was eighteen or twenty-eight, but I knew it was going to happen."

Returning to his working-class Richmond neighborhood to woodshed in his bedroom, D'Angelo was focused. "It was frustrating at times," he remembered. "I was trying to find myself and experimenting a lot while attempting to come up with my own sound, something that I could call mine."

At the time, D'Angelo was helping a crew of local rappers called I.D.U. (Intelligent, Deadly, Unique), making beats for them to perform to. "That's how I started working the fusion of hip-hop and soul and got that smooth but rugged sound," he explained. "Everything I did, I played it for my cousins and got their feedback."

Sleeping in the daytime and recording through the night, D sometimes chilled out watching kung fu flicks or listening to blaxploitation soundtracks by Willie Hutch (*The Mack*),

Roy Ayers (*Coffy*), and James Brown (*Slaughter's Big Rip-Off*). Nevertheless, the main objective was making music. "Sometimes, I would burn incense or candles, but sometimes I don't need that shit, because the vibe is already there. Once you got that feeling, anything could work." A few of the songs on *Brown Sugar* were demo'd in his bedroom studio, including "Smooth," "Higher," "Alright," and "Me and Those Dreamin' Eyes of Mine."

Yet when I mentioned that the upbeat track "When We Get By" was a favorite, D'Angelo smiled. "Most of the songs are dark, but that one has a blue-skies kind of atmosphere to it," he replied.

"Especially when compared to a track like 'Shit, Damn, Motherfucker,'" I countered. "What would make you write a song about a guy murdering his best friend for sleeping with his woman?"

D'Angelo smirked. "Man, where I'm from, stuff like that happens all the time. Then you look at TV and you see O.J. or that Lorena Bobbitt shit. Can't deny that there is a thin line between love and hate. When it comes to songwriting, I modeled myself after Stevie Wonder. Sometimes you put poetry to beautiful music, and other times you got to come direct. A song like 'Shit, Damn, Motherfucker' is just a sign of the times."

"Do you keep a notebook?"

"Nah, I have a pretty good memory. When I'm writing songs, I usually just trust my brain. I start with my music and build the song from there." More than a few of the *Brown Sugar* tracks were inspired by an ex-girlfriend. "The first song I wrote for her was 'Alright.' Man, my feelings for her were so deep. Instead of writing letters, I gave her songs. By writing songs for her, I compiled the material that became my demos."

After finishing the *Brown Sugar* demos, D'Angelo sent tapes to a talent scout in Texas. "He told me I needed some work, so I soon left Richmond and drove to New York City with two hundred dollars in my pocket and a place to stay in Brooklyn." Giving the same material to Midnight Music publisher Jocelyn Cooper, the country boy soon received seven offers from major record companies.

It was also during this period that D'Angelo befriended A Tribe Called Quest, whom he credited with looking out for him during his transitional period between moving to the city and completing *Brown Sugar*. "That was when they were finishing up the *Midnight Marauders* album," explained D. "I was eighteen and didn't know shit. Tribe schooled me. I didn't know anything about the business or New York."

Says former EMI executive Gary Harris, "Originally, I had thought about recruiting [former Motown/Marvin Gaye producer] Leon Ware to produce the album. We had talked about doing an album that was reminiscent of Marvin's *I Want You* album, which Ware was a major collaborator. Instead, D'Angelo went away and made *Brown Sugar*, which was the end of that decision."

While D'Angelo might've entertained the idea of using the veteran Motown producer (in the same way that Earth, Wind & Fire founder Maurice White was once considered as a producer for Prince's debut), the piano player had his own musical visions. "People forget that music should be artful," D'Angelo philosophized. "There is a difference between artists and stars. For me, what comes first is the music. I want to make dope music. It's been like that from the beginning, and it's going to stay like that."

After two hours of chatter that Sunday afternoon, D'Angelo took one last cigarette from the depleted pack. Lighting up in the restaurant doorway, he offered to drive me home.

Walking a few blocks in the drizzle to his messy ride parked inside a garage, D'Angelo slid behind the wheel and looked around on the floor until he located a cassette of Marvin's least celebrated masterpiece, *Here, My Dear*.

"One of the reasons I like Marvin Gaye so much—he didn't give a fuck," D'Angelo explained, putting the tape into the deck. "He just said whatever the fuck he wanted to say, but he did it so dope, motherfuckers had to appreciate. He was an artist, a true artist."

D'Angelo was all of ten years old when his future hero was blasted by his own minister daddy on April Fools' Day 1984. "It was a Sunday, and we were coming home from church," D'Angelo said. "We stopped at my cousin's house, and the first thing he said was, 'Yo, Marvin Gaye got killed by his father.' I thought he was joking. After that, I had nightmares for years. Finally, I had to go to a shrink, and she broke the whole thing down for me. His father was a preacher, and my father was a preacher. I can't explain what happened, but one day I was able to listen to his voice without being petrified. I can't explain that either."

As we got to my block, I glanced at the future of soul and wondered aloud how he might deal with fame if *Brown Sugar* became a smash. "You might not be able to sit up in restaurants and drive writers home," I joked.

Glaring sullenly as though I was full of shit, D'Angelo seemed to think there was no way he would possibly be R&B's next great superstar. "I'll take it day by day," D assured me.

Double-parking his ride in front of my building, D'Angelo mumbled, "Thank you, man," as Marvin Gaye continued to sing. Driving away, he had no idea that his life would never be so simple again. ○

follow music making tech
daily, free and open

createdigitalmusic.com

king britt, by grace bastidas

GOOD RECORDS NYC

BUY | SELL | TRADE

Soul, Jazz, Rock, Hip-Hop, Afro, Disco, Latin, Brazillian, & Everything Else

218 E. 5th Street, NYC

Shop on our new web site:
www.goodrecordsnyc.com

Rene Lopez

Hot New EP
"Johnny Wants to be a Matador"

Full length CD
"People Are Just People"

AVAILABLE NOW
purchase both at www.renelopez.com
CATCH RENE ON TOUR 2010

Legend

Del Casher: Guitarist, music composer, inventor, and consultant to Thomas Organ Co. during the invention of the wah-wah pedal. Casher is the first guitarist to play the wah-wah on a recording session, adding the distinctive sound to the scores of Vic Mizzy in films like *The Shakiest Gun in the West* and *The Ghost and Mr. Chicken*.

Dennis Coffey: Detroit session guitarist and composer. Coffey brought effects pedals to R&B music with his use of the wah-wah pedal on "Cloud Nine" by the Temptations at Motown Records.

Leroy "Sugarfoot" Bonner: Singer, guitarist, and songwriter with the Ohio Players, whose Westbound albums were drenched in wah-wah.

Bobby Eli: Guitarist and songwriter primarily known for doing sessions in Philadelphia as part of MFSB, the session musicians who recorded for Kenny Gamble and Leon Huff at Philadelphia International Records. Eli wrote "Love Won't Let Me Wait" for Major Harris, "Sideshow" for Blue Magic, and "Just Don't Want to Be Lonely" for the Main Ingredient.

Charles "Skip" Pitts: Session guitarist with the Isley Brothers ("It's Your Thing"), as well as for Stax Records. Pitts can be heard on Isaac Hayes's seminal *Shaft* theme.

Craig McMullen: Guitarist with Curtis Mayfield (*Super Fly*); did sessions with Donald Byrd, Freddie Hubbard, and Marlena Shaw.

Pete Carr: Session guitarist at Muscle Shoals Studio. Carr played lead guitar on hits by Luther Ingram—"(If Loving You Is Wrong) I Don't Want to Be Right"—and Rod Stewart.

Wayne Kramer: Guitarist, singer, and songwriter with the MC5, the Detroit proto-punk group. Kramer played on the first two Was (Not Was) albums.

John Tropea: New York session guitarist, solo artist. Played on Deodato's CTI albums, including on the songs "September 13," "Super Strut," and "Also Sprach Zarathustra."

Leo Nocentelli: Guitarist, singer, and songwriter from New Orleans; member of the Meters.

Jim McCarty: Guitarist with Mitch Ryder and the Detroit Wheels, the Buddy Miles Express, Cactus, and the Rockets. A friend of Jimi Hendrix, McCarty appears with Hendrix on one posthumously released recording, *Nine to the Universe*.

Photo courtesy of Del Casher.

I began playing guitar with the Four Tops on the third of September, 1991, in Las Vegas. The group was booked with the Temptations in a package sold as "TNT" (Temps 'n' Tops). At the start of the show, both groups would appear together onstage and engage in a sort of mock battle. Part of the gig involved covering the classic wah-wah figures on the songs by the Temptations. The five years I spent on the road gave me an appreciation and a lingering curiosity about the wah-wah. I saw firsthand how audiences responded to the sound; its effect is transcendent. I wondered when, where, how, and why it was created. I wanted to talk to the players who established the language, the guitarists who, like me, owe some portion of gratitude to the wah-wah pedal.

So, from Vegas, let's travel west across the desert and farther back in time. It's 1967, the Godfather of Soul is in the factory of the Thomas Organ Co. in Sepulveda, California. Del Casher, a consultant, is playing his guitar through the prototype wah-wah and making his best pitch. Casher was born in Indiana, a sort of whiz kid. While still in his teens, he hosted a radio show and met and impressed his idol, Les Paul. By 1958, the twenty-year-old had moved to Hollywood where he played on *The Lawrence Welk Show* and eventually appeared in the film *Roustabout* with Elvis Presley. Casher remembers vividly the day he met with JB, "I thought, this is the thing for soul music, because you can really express yourself. Who would be better to show this wah-wah pedal than James Brown? He's gonna put this thing on the map. [*points to photo*] I'm begging him at that point. 'Please reconsider the wah-wah pedal, please, James, please!'" It seems difficult to believe. Perhaps Casher's enthusiasm and hard-sell delivery were too much. In any event, JB was not alone. The wah-wah was born of chance and irony, its life marked by complexity and contradiction.

The story begins with the Vox AC30 amplifier made in England. Dick Denney, a British guitarist and engineer, had added a midrange boost (MRB) switch to the amp. (The wah-wah effect is produced by scrolling through the midrange frequencies that resemble the formants of human speech.) Because the Beatles endorsed Vox, the Thomas Organ Co. made a deal with the British company to distribute their products in America. Thomas Organ decided to build the amps in California and to cut costs began transforming them from vacuum-tube technology to solid-state (transistor) technology. (It's worth noting that most guitar players prefer tubes to transistors, and this decision may have led to a decline in the Vox reputation and eventual bankruptcy.) In late 1966, solid-state engineer Brad Plunkett, whose name appears on the wah-wah patent, was assigned the task of converting the MRB switch for the new American Vox amps. The *wah* would soon be discovered.

Del Casher: During that transformation, I got involved with the Vox Ampliphonic Orchestra, which was part of the big plan to have an electric amplifier orchestra perform and represent the Vox products. They wanted to sell amplifiers. Brad had converted the MRB switch to a variable potentiometer

Del Casher using the Wah Wah pedal for the first time in a recording session. Photo courtesy of Del Casher/Cache Agency.

because it was going to save some money. As I was playing it, I realized it made an amazing human-voice sound. It reminded me of when I was eight years old: I heard Gene Autry's harmonica player who, with his cupped hands, could make the harmonica talk. He made the harmonica sound like a baby crying. He was saying, "I want my mama, wah-wah."

I immediately asked the head of Vox engineering, Stan Cutler, "Can we get this circuit into a pedal?" He said sure, so we grabbed a volume control from a Vox Continental Organ—it was just a plain old gray pedal—and they slammed the circuit in. The story has it that someone plugged the guitar into the pedal. Well, that someone was me. I was saying, "We gotta do this." I was consulting with them, and I was working all kinds of record dates. I thought this was something that was going to be revolutionary. You have to remember at that time, 1966, excepting the Japanese transistor radios, everything plugged into the wall. So to be able to take a circuit and put a nine-volt battery to it, an active circuit, is the key thing. That was similar to a mixing console in a studio. It was unheard of, it was phenomenal.

Dennis Coffey: Hendrix and Clapton were using it before me, but I was the first one to use it on an R&B record, on "Cloud Nine" with the Temptations. I had a friend—a guitar player who I went to high school with by the name of Joe Podorsek—he had a place called Capitol Music. I used to go in there to buy stuff, to get my guitars maintained. Joe was very good, he was a salesman, he'd say, "Hey, here's something new; it just came in. Take a listen to it; borrow it to try it out." So he was constantly feeding me new products.

Leroy "Sugarfoot" Bonner: That was the only thing we had [back then]. [*laughs*] Truly. You had fuzz and wah-wah. You had the Echoplex, but that was too complex for people to be using. So the wah-wah pedal started being the most commonly used pedal of all pedals that have ever been made. And the wah-wah still is the most commonly used, that and the fuzz tone. I had every kind, [Maestro] Boomerang, Vox wah-wah. I was a regular guitar person back in those days; if it was equipment, I had to have it.

Bobby Eli: Although I do more than that, I've been tagged as the wah-wah/effects specialist. I've always been a gadget man, even when I was coming up as a kid. I liked to tinker with things, push buttons, and make things happen. So when electric guitar sound-effects pedals came on the market, I started buying stuff, making connections at music stores. One thing led to another, and I was labeled as the electronic guy. As a matter of fact, Salsoul Records used to credit me on the back of album covers as Bobby "Electronic" Eli, so that kind of stuck. I liked that, because it gave me an identity apart from Norman Harris who was the Wes Montgomery kind of mellow guy.

For my bar mitzvah, my parents bought me a brand-new Les Paul, which I wish I still had. It was a goldtop, and if I still had it in the condition it was in at that time, it would be worth a ton of money. But me being a kid, I sanded it down, painted it, put glitter on it, sanded the glitter off, painted it this horrible red. What did I know? Was I a prophet? I loved that guitar, but I guess I didn't love it enough not to mess with it. I don't think the whole hookup, even with the amp, was more than five hundred bucks. On the way home from the store—because I had gone down there to pick the guitar and amp up on the bus, right—I also bought a pizza. So the pizza juice spilled on the grill the first day—all over—typical of stuff that happens to me; I'm so clumsy sometimes.

Del Casher: Now an interesting side line to this whole story was Joe Benaron, who was the CEO, came rushing in, and the minute he heard me do this with the guitar, he said, "Oh my gosh, we can put this on trumpets." The very first ads that came out, which was not my preference, were saying your trumpet can sound like Clyde McCoy. That was my silly joke to Joe Benaron: "If you want to put out a wah-wah pedal for trumpet, why don't you call it Clyde McCoy?" And that's what they did. Clyde McCoy's name went on the pedal much to my disappointment, not because I wanted my name on the pedal, but because Clyde McCoy had nothing to do with it. They were old men living in the past.

Charles "Skip" Pitts: I don't like no tinny sound. I loved the Boomerang; I'd love to have another one. I gave [the Stax Museum] my only one. My first wife [Eula Jean Rivers], she knew Isaac [Hayes] years ago. She was in a group called the Charmels, and he was trying to record at Stax before he even got big. I was going with her while I was with the Isley Brothers. [Hayes] came to the Apollo, and I didn't go up there; I didn't know him. So Jean, my first wife, went up and told him she went with me, and I did "It's Your Thing." He said, "Oh, I dig that. I wanna talk to him, because I'm gettin' me a new band, and I like what I heard."

On "Never Can Say Goodbye" [from *Black Moses*], you notice I'm not puttin' none of my stuff in it, 'cause I wasn't that comfortable yet—just what he asked me to play. He loved it. *Black Moses* was the first album [I played on].

Me and Michael [Toles were on "Theme from *Shaft*"]. I made the lead [wah] and Michael did the [rhythm] wah-wah. When you see the liner notes, it says the Movement and the Bar-Kays—the only Bar-Kays that was there was James Alexander and Michael Toles. The rest of the guys were in his band: Me, Willie Hall, Lester Snell, and Onzie Horne.

Craig McMullen: I had the [Vox] Cry Baby earlier—before

I got with Curtis. With the Impressions, I didn't have to use it that much, but, eventually, when Curtis went solo, I had to find another one, and I went with the Vox. They were basically about the same. I used to do little trick things to it to personalize it, to make the distance between the treble and the bass sound go a little quicker. We cut the soundtrack to *Super Fly* in ['71], and the actual movie release was in ['72].

Leo Nocentelli: [When] I purchased a wah-wah, it was kind of new on the scene. And the first time I used it was on a song called "Here Comes the Meter Man." I think it was a Cry Baby way back then. I kept continuously using it for a while, and then it got lost in the fact that everybody was using it. Then it took a hiatus—people stopped using it. It seemed like a piece of equipment that wasn't consistent. Now it seems like the wah-wah is really prevalent in a lot of music that you hear. Like everybody knows, when Hendrix came out, everybody started patterning themselves after him. He was one of the first guys of notoriety that did certain things with the wah-wah. What he did brought the wah-wah into prominence.

Del Casher: I said, "Joe, before you go too far with this whole deal, let me make a Vox demo record of the guitar." He literally told me, "Well, there's no money in that." He said, "Look, you're the only guitar player in this band, and I got four trumpet players and four saxophone players, four trombones. Look, right off the bat, I can sell twelve pedals to all the guys in the band, because they all have a little amplifier in front of them." His economics was logical, but he was very illogical, because we weren't going back to big bands. I said, "Please let me make a Vox demo record to show guitar players what can be done with the wah-wah pedal." So he agreed to pay me, and I put it out in my garage studio with a drummer, and I overdubbed all the parts, the Vox demo record. And he had such low confidence that the wah-wah was gonna be for the guitar that they put it out, instead of on a vinyl 45 record, he put it out on a cardboard plastic record; you play it twice and it was gone. Joe didn't want to spend any money on it; there was just no faith in the fact that the guitar was the target of the wah-wah pedal. Now this is hard to believe, isn't it?

Bobby Eli: I was playing in a band called Herb Johnson and the Impacts. We were a bar band; we did frat parties and stuff like that. So we were working at a place called Scotty's Bar on Fifty-second Street, in West Philly. This guy Kenny [Gamble] used to come in and kind of do a walk onstage and sing. He'd do a Jerry Butler or Marvin Gaye song or whatever. He noticed that I knew all the songs. Then we struck up a conversation, and he was basically a lab tech at a hospital who dabbled in music on the side and sang. And Leon Huff, I actually met a couple of years earlier. He was a piano player with a group called the Lavenders. I was in Huff's apartment one day; I had a vocal group I was working with over there. Huff lived in the projects in Camden at the time. We went over there, my guitar and the singing group. I was playing away. The phone rang. I heard Huff talking away to somebody on the phone: "Hey, man, there's this bad White boy over here, Bobby Eli. Man, he's playing his ass off. You should check him out." Right after, they started working with the Intruders, and so I did some sessions here and there—not on a regular basis until maybe '68 when Sigma [Sound Studios] actually first opened. I was there the day Kenny Gamble said [to Sigma owner/engineer Joe Tarsia], "Sounds great, Joe, we'll use it." They did a demo session. From then on in, I guess, I was elected. I was there from the beginning. I mean, I didn't make every single session, but ninety-eight percent of 'em.

I had a Cry Baby. I mainly did my thing. In fact, a lot of disco records such as "Turn the Beat Around" just copied what I did for the most part. The Philly wah-wah thing was different than the "Shaft" thing and what Dennis Coffey did with the Temps. My strokes were much tighter and more choked than that of my contemporaries. I sometimes combined the wah-wah with an Echoplex on a lot of ballads. I also used the "cricket" effect whereby I did arpeggios near the bridge while muting the strings with my palm with the wah-wah pressed midway down while the Echoplex was going. You can hear the effect on "Who Am I" by the O'Jays. Some of my favorites are [the O'Jays'] "For the Love of Money," [MFSB's] "Sexy," [William DeVaughn's] "Be Thankful for What You Got," [Harold Melvin's] "Hope That We Can Be Together Soon," [and the O'Jays'] "I Love Music."

Dennis Coffey: My gear for the Motown stuff started with that wah-wah pedal, and I did all the Temptations stuff: "Psychedelic Shack," "Can't Get Next to You," all the records they did including the introduction to "Just My Imagination." That was pretty straight, that tune. The only thing I didn't do was "Papa Was a Rollin' Stone," because I was out with "Scorpio." Wah Wah Watson was on the road, and they brought him in to do some stuff, so we did some things together, and I showed him the wah-wah pedal. And he of course ended up using it and getting a little space for himself.

Del Casher: The record was released February 1, 1967. Ironically, the patent that Vox had with Brad Plunkett's name was applied for February 23, 1967. The wah-wah I'm talking about is my prototype with the gray finish. It was never released as a commercial pedal; that was the chrome pedal that said Clyde McCoy on the bottom, the 846. My pedal was hand-wired with me leaning over the bench and asking to have certain parts altered—the capacitors and resistors—because the Dick

Denney circuit was very harsh. When you went down on the pedal, it was like glass shattering. Brad Plunkett was just following orders; he had nothing to do with the musicality. He transistorized the circuit that Dick Denny designed. When you say inventor, you've got to put a whole lot of names in there: Dick Denney, MRB switch; Brad Plunkett, transistor genius who converted; Del Casher who said, "This is amazing. We gotta put this into a pedal."

Pete Carr: I used the wah-wah on a few things. It was never a staple, exactly. I believe it was a Cry Baby—but I'm not sure—way back then on [Luther Ingram's "If Loving You Is Wrong"]. It just struck me it would be good for the part. Like usual, they would sing the song with acoustic guitar or somethin', and we would come up with the parts—you know, rearrange it and actually make a record out of it. That's kind of how we worked. That's kind of why people came to us, because we could take somethin' real raw, and we were all pretty good at coming up with arrangements to make whatever somebody had, a rough body of a song, and turn it into a record.

I remember [Ingram's crew] comin' in; it was kind of a trip watchin' those dudes. One had a gun, and also one would jump down on the floor and do about fifty push-ups and jump back up—kind of rough guys, almost like gangsters. Luther Ingram himself was super talented, I loved him. He was a great songwriter and singer.

Leroy "Sugarfoot" Bonner: I even did ["Skin Tight"] with fuzz [first]. I did it on everything, flat-out to see which had the best effect. The wah-wah had the best effect. It had a humanistic flow to it, you know what I mean? It had more of a humanness about it than just a straight-sounding guitar. Humans vibrate; they have vibes. Voices come in tones. Your voice changes from high pitches to low pitches. It gives you that alive feeling. It makes you feel like something is crawling around you, moving around. Because the sound is moving, you feel the movement. You can have a wah-wah on keyboard, but it's no way as effective as in a pedal [with guitar]. That sound is always going to be with us, because it adds that humanness to the music.

Del Casher: [Once we had the prototype, I went to] the R&D department, saying, "This is great, but it's not good enough." I went to Stan Cutler, the head of the R&D department, and I said, "Stan, you gotta let me borrow one of your guys so I can make this thing sound right." He said, "Well, go talk to Brad." [Brad] said, "What do you want me to do?" I said, "Change this capacitor, change this, let's try it." I distinctly remember, because it was wintertime, like nine o'clock in the morning, driving him and that R&D department absolutely crazy. When we finally got it to sound right, it was four in the afternoon. That's when Joe Benaron walked in, and I said, "This is it, Joe. This is what we need for the guitar."

Wayne Kramer: Today, it's just part of the language of the electric guitar. It's in the arsenal, one of the ways to process sound. I used the fuzz tone; I had a bunch of those, but my thing with all those stomp boxes and gear, mentally, is that it's just more stuff to go wrong. It's more stuff to break in the middle of the set, which ruins the flow of the performance. I've traditionally been reluctant to embrace that stuff, maybe it's because I dance so much when I play. I'm more concerned with trying to get from this note to the other note, this chord to the other chord, to play something in the moment that is heartfelt. A lot of just being a player is, you know, trying to get through the night with as little damage as possible. Generally, I'm not inarticulate, but I'm actually kind of at a loss for much to say about it. Maybe I'm not the right guy to interview. [*laughs*]

Dennis Coffey: Here's my thing on the effects. Back in the day when I was with the Royaltones, I had a thing called an Echoplex. We were actually using it for tape delay for the PA. I ended up running guitar through it, and you hear that on "In the Rain" by the Dramatics, which was probably the first time that was used on an R&B record. And then I had a Tone Bender, which was a Vox distortion device. Anything that makes the guitar sound bigger, I like. That's why Les Paul was, to me, such an idol. Because he kept playing at ninety-three, plus all of his multitracking and inventions, he was obviously into things that make the guitar sound better. That's kind of my approach, and I'm still looking.

Charles "Skip" Pitts: Back in the '70s, all they wanted was "Shaft." Anytime Isaac had to take a flight and do a TV show or somethin', I'm the only one he took in the band, because he had to have "Shaft" played right. We'd meet the band at the next gig. I'm not braggin'; I'm just tellin' you true shit. I didn't get my just due for it. Had I known it was going to do what it did, I would have had some negotiating to do. Ironically, after we did that, Isaac said, "Well, man, they want me to do a sequel, and I'm gonna give you some points and more play on it." And then the writer Gordon Parks didn't let Isaac do it. What happened is, [Johnny Pate] ended up doin' the music to *Shaft in Africa*. Well, it didn't do nothin.' You don't ever hear it anymore on TV or nothin'.

Del Casher: They treated me very, very well. They paid me very well for the demo record. They paid me for the press conferences. We didn't see the pedal as an invention; that's why it came as a shock to me. I never bothered to look up the U.S. patent. It came as a shock to me to realize that Joe Benaron had jumped on it and had a patent applied for and put Brad's name on it. And Les Kushner, I have no idea what he thinks he did with that, because he was standing around doing noth-

ing with it—they put his name on it as well. I always want to give tremendous credit to Brad Plunkett for being such an advanced solid-state engineer.

Craig McMullen: When I'm doin' wah-wah parts, I'm goin' in and out. In other words, I'm only puttin' the wah-wah in on certain things, and then I'll go back to playin' rhythm or play lead lines—whatever it would take at the time. Curtis always depended on you to make up somethin' to go along. He just gives you an idea of what he's going to do, and then you would counter it with something that would be advantageous to the track. You had the freedom to make up your own parts. My licks was licks that I created myself to go along with what the situation was. We were all kind of close-knit, so we could feel each other. It was a good setting. It worked especially for us three [Curtis, myself, and the bassist], what you would call the melodic players. We very seldom bumped heads; we had that cohesiveness. It helped me out when I started living in L.A.—I started doing other sessions; a lot of times you're playing with two guitar players, or sometimes even three. You wanna make sure you put your licks [in the right place], so you don't get them put on the cutting-room floor. [*laughs*] It becomes a team thing. You listen to the other guys and make sure you come up with a hit track, 'cause that's what the producers are looking for.

John Tropea: The reason I bought a wah-wah is, in [1969], "Cissy Strut" [b/w "Here Comes the Meter Man"] became popular. Shortly after that, I bought the Vox.

I got a call to do a demo one afternoon; it was for an Astrud Gilberto record. It's a funny thing, because there was a very bad storm that day. I almost canceled because it was so bad. I decided to go in anyway, because in those days, I wasn't all that busy. I go in and it's Deodato [at the helm]. I did the date, and about two or three weeks later, I get a call from Creed Taylor, and he wants me to record, booking me on these dates for Deodato. So that led to playing on his record [*Prelude*, which included the hit "Also Sprach Zarathustra"]. It was one of those real bad spring storms; all the trees were coming down. It's kind of funny, because if I didn't do that [Gilberto date], where would I be today?

Creed Taylor was a good producer as far as I'm concerned. He wasn't really one of those guys who gets involved with what you're playing. He was very quiet about it and let you do your thing. If he didn't like something, he'd say, "Why don't you try a different sound?" or somethin'. But he wasn't intrusive. Van Gelder is a dynamite engineer, and he's a man not without quirks. The studio was spotless. One time, Deodato and I took a break for lunch, and we were sitting out in the recording area. I ordered a big milkshake and a hamburger. I put it on a little ashtray thing with a stand. I went to open the milkshake and the milkshake fell because the stand was flimsy. It fell all over the floor. Deodato looks at me and says in his Brazilian-English accent, "Oh, Tropea, now you in trouble." And I looked in the control room; Van Gelder was seething. Now we're trying not to laugh, you know. We all scurried to clean it up.

Del Casher: The pedal was difficult for me to get launched. The record industry didn't see any application for the pedal when I showed it to them. The film people loved it. They didn't see it as a blues or soul thing; that's the only disappointment I had with them. The Thomas Organ Co. had a ton of money to spend; they just spent it the wrong way. The only outcome out of the whole Vox episode was this little bit of serendipity, when Joe Benaron said, "Let's save some money on Dick Denney's MRB switch, make it a variable pot," which Brad Plunkett did. Don't get me wrong, credit should be given to Brad, but I think Del's name should have been on the patent. But, I'm not bitter about it, the patent only lasts seventeen years. Nobody is making any money; this is all based on historical accuracy. It wasn't something where a mad scientist sat down in candlelight and said, "Aha, I'm going to invent the wah-wah pedal." I had that wah-wah pedal part of 1966, all of 1967. In 1968, Vox went bankrupt. I thought it was the most disastrous idea I ever came up with. And then Hendrix went on [at] Woodstock in 1969.

Jim McCarty: I used a Vox Cry Baby. That's what everyone was using at the time. I first heard it on Hendrix's second album, *Axis: Bold as Love*—the second song, "Up From the Skies." Clapton was playing it too, but Jimi was better. He was better at everything; the guy was a genius. Clapton would use it with the meter of the tune; Hendrix used it depending on the note. He could make it sound like he was talking. When I was with Buddy Miles, I ran into him on a regular basis. I was on the first two albums: *Expressway to Your Skull* and *Electric Church*. I think I only used the wah-wah on a couple of tunes. Jimi produced half of that second album. He was hanging around the band a lot and talking to Buddy about putting something together [which would become Band of Gypsys]. There's an album, *Nine to the Universe*, [with] a tune called the "Jimi/Jimmy Jam" with me and him playing. I was in awe of the guy.

Charles "Skip" Pitts: I knew Jimi. They were playin' behind a guy named Gorgeous George. I was with Gene Chandler. We had a tour; they weren't givin' us shit, but I wanted to be there. Gorgeous George was the master of ceremony, but he only sung one song in the middle of the show, "Please, Please, Please." He hired Jimi for five dollars, and Jimi got all the women; they ran past George and right to him, because he was doin' all this [*puts air guitar behind head*]. He was very bashful until he got onstage. He didn't talk to nobody much. He'd

Conscientious Observer

Songwriter Ernie Hines instilled his music with messages to the world

by **Daniel Margolis**

In his five decades in music, Ernie Hines has made some pretty spectacular connections. Playing with Slim Harpo, L. C. Cook, and Pervis Staples. Working with director Otto Preminger. Performing at Wattstax. And getting sampled on Pete Rock & C.L. Smooth's *Mecca and the Soul Brother* without even knowing it. His early singles for Chess and his debut album for We Produce, a subsidiary of Stax Records, saw him backed by a cast of esteemed musicians, but record company fallouts kept his work from being properly promoted or even released at all. Nevertheless, the music persists, and Hines's story is that of a man demonstrating impressive resilience during a lifelong career in the industry.

Ernie Hines was born in Jackson, Mississippi, on August 8, 1938. "From an early age, music was always in our home," says Hines. "My mother was a Christian, and she brought me to the Lord early on. And my grandmother on my father's side was a choir singer. I get that from her. But the ability to draw, which I recognize as my first God-given talent, was why I moved during junior high school to Duluth, Minnesota. To pursue an art career." There, Hines's uncle had a gospel quartet, which drew the young artist back into singing. Hines also became involved with sports, playing with a semipro baseball team and on his high school and college football teams upon returning to Jackson.

Hines had also taken up guitar by this point and would soon marry, drop out of college, and move to Baton Rouge, Louisiana, where he would gig with gospel groups and work at Wolf's Bakery, a well-known establishment in town. Through another bakery employee, Hines was enlisted by the Scotland-Aires, a group that recorded a radio commercial for the bakery and in the process became "a household word, the top group in Baton Rouge," explains Hines.

Work with the Scotland-Aires got Hines noticed by a Chicago DJ named Alvin "Diggie Doo" Dixon, who referred Hines

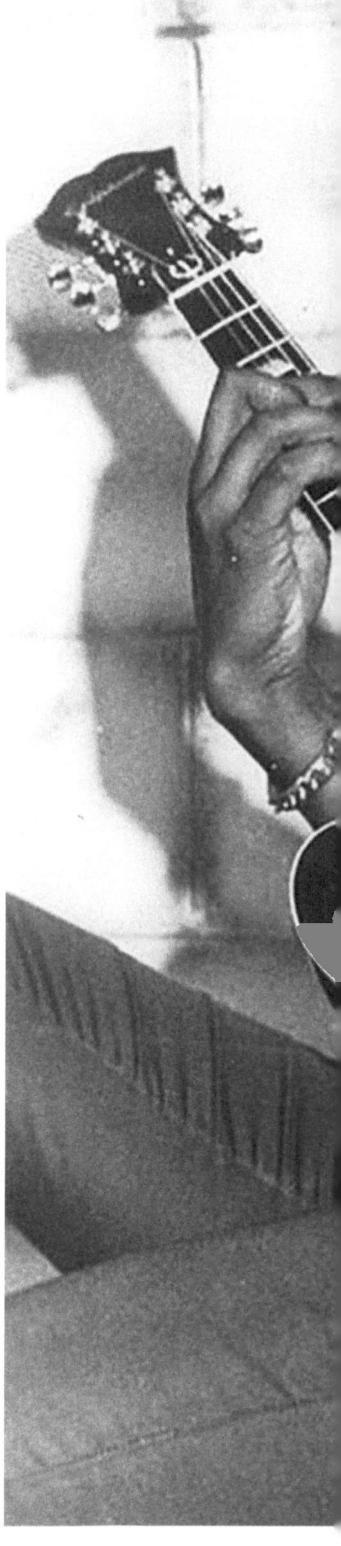

Ernie Hines, 1964.
Photo courtesy of Ernie Hines.

(*clockwise from top left*) Ernie Hines and L. C. Cooke, 1964. Ernie Hines and Don Cornelius on *Soul Train*. Ernie with *Shaft* star Richard Roundtree at Wattstax. Hines with Quincy Jones at the Black Expo, 1972. L. C. Cooke, Ernie Hines, and Johnny Taylor, 1968. Joe Valentine's Band, 1965. Photos courtesy of Ernie Hines.

for work backing gospel, blues, R&B, and soul luminaries like Slim Harpo, Lowell Fulson, Clyde McPhatter, Johnnie Taylor, and L. C. Cook, the younger brother of Sam Cooke. This last connection would prove to be particularly fortuitous for Hines, nudging him out of Baton Rouge and onto the road.

"L.C. had a big hit song out on SAR Records called 'Put Me Down Easy,'" says Hines. "Diggie knew the Cook family because he was from Gary and was in and out of Chicago. So when L.C. came into town, Diggie said, 'I have just the guitarist for you, and once you hear him, you're going to want to take him on the road with you.'"

Hines quit his bakery job and headed to Miami with Cook. "We were in and out of Miami quite a bit after that," says Hines. "We did the same way Sam did. Sam would go into a place with Cliff White, his guitarist, and they would hire a band. We would do the same thing with L.C. So in Miami, we would have a band working with us, and I would conduct the band and rehearse the songs and everything for the gig."

News of the death of Sam Cooke in December 1964 dislodged this working arrangement. Hines—who had been married to his second wife, Jill, by the Reverend Charles Cook, Sam and L.C.'s father—went to Chicago for a memorial service and then returned to Baton Rouge, hooking up with Joe Valentine for an engagement in Houston.

Back in Baton Rouge, Hines reported to a local hotel known as "a hangout for musicians." There, Hines learned that he was being sought out by director Otto Preminger and composer Hugo Montenegro, in town to film the movie *Hurry Sundown*, a racially charged film set just after World War II starring Michael Caine, Jane Fonda, Faye Dunaway, and Burgess Meredith. "Someone had recommended me because they were looking for a guitarist to do some music on the set," says Hines.

Hines performed the film's theme during shooting in summer 1966 to assist in its integration into the film. His playing is not featured in the movie, though it was recorded. Hines also taught actor Robert Hooks to pantomime the film's theme on guitar. "I'm in some of those scenes too," says Hines. "It was exciting, because at that time, Robert Hooks, Diahann Carroll, John Phillip Law, Frank Converse, Beah Richards, and George Kennedy, they were virtually unknown actors."

Chess Players

After shooting on *Hurry Sundown* wrapped, Hines stayed in Baton Rouge and ran into Roscoe Robinson, a well-known gospel singer who traveled in the same circles as Hines.

"He said, 'Pete'—that's a name we got in the habit of calling each other," remembers Hines. "When we were on the road with L.C., it was always 'Pete this' or 'Pete that,' and everyone was Pete. Roscoe said, 'Pete, man, if you come to Chicago, I'll record you.'"

Hines moved to Chicago where he and Robinson hooked up with Sonny Thompson, a bandleader and songwriter best known for the song "Drown in My Own Tears," a 1956 hit for Ray Charles. "Sonny was a mainstay," says Hines. "A pianist extraordinaire at Chess Records. He worked with rock-and-roll bands."

At Chess, Robinson and Thompson recorded four songs written and performed by Hines: "We're Gonna Party," "Thank You Baby (For a Love Beyond Compare)," "Rain, Rain, Rain," and "Sincerely Mine." In gratitude, Hines gave songwriting credit on all four tracks to Thompson. These songs were supposed to be released on the New York label Scepter Records, but after a falling out between Robinson and Scepter, Hines leased the songs to USA Records, which released them as two separate singles in 1968.

The songs themselves are bright, propulsive, pop R&B, with Hines on guitar. He is accompanied by a capable rhythm section, horns, and a chorus of female backup singers delivering lines like "We'll have cheese on the moon/And the band will play our favorite tune/And then we'll follow the dipper to the rainbow end" with admirable conviction. Regardless, the record company shuffle meant these singles went relatively unnoticed. During this same period, Hines wrote songs for gospel group the Violinaires and for R&B acts Little Ben and the Cheers, and the Lovelites.

Going Down to Stax

Hines's next move came through his wife's job as an administrative assistant in the advertising department at Johnson Publishing Company. Johnson's founder, John H. Johnson, "had connections," says Hines, "because he had *Black Stars*, *Ebony*, *Jet*, you know. It's a big publishing company. [Johnson] knew I was in the business, and he always would try to help my career along, so he put me in touch with Al Bell, and they flew me down to listen to some of my music."

Hines brought demos and a guitar to Stax Records in Memphis and played his songs "Help Me Put Out the Flame (In My Heart)," "A Better World (For Everyone)," and "I Can't Stand the Pain" for Bell and others. "They were impressed with the music, and so he signed me," says Hines. The former two songs were quickly recorded and released in 1970; Stax passed on the latter. "I couldn't understand why they kept that in the can and never did anything with it," says Hines.

Ernie Hines, Stax Press, 1972. Photo courtesy of Ernie Hines.

Hines then recorded two more singles, released on the Stax subsidiary We Produce: "Electrified Love" b/w "Come on Y'all" and "What Would I Do" b/w "Our Generation." Signing to Stax afforded him access to some stellar backing musicians. "We recorded there at the Memphis studio with some of the MGs and some of the [musicians who] played with Otis Redding," says Hines. "It was like a family group. Like Motown."

These sessions included contributions from bassist Donald "Duck" Dunn, keyboardist Marvell Thomas, and various members of the Bar-Kays. Recording these initial singles for Stax stretched into sessions for Hines's debut album, *Electrified*. The basic tracks were completed in Memphis with some overdubbing done in Chicago and Detroit.

The album kicks off with "Electrified Love," a warm, midtempo ballad penned by Hines's drummer, Leon Triplett. It also boasts a cover of "A Change Is Gonna Come," as "a memorial to Sam," explains Hines.

Cooke's message of overcoming adversity for a better existence sat well with much of the other material on *Electrified*. On "A Better World (For Everyone)," Hines laments the declining state of human capital in the early '70s: "People are talking about these changing times/And how it's gotten so a man's life ain't worth a dime."

"It was my thinking about the world—it was my message," says Hines. "From time to time, those kind of songs have fallen on me, and I have to pick up the pen and put it down."

"Come On Y'all" finds Hines—backed by dark, stirring strings, a chorus of male backup singers, sparsely placed bass, and his own quietly chugging rhythm guitar—exhorting the listener to join him in an idyllic sanctuary built up to an unbelievable degree before it's eventually revealed as merely "the neighborhood hall."

"Come On," along with three other songs on the album, was written by a Chicago schoolteacher named Leon Moore, who had been contracted by the album's producer, Tom Nixon. "I've tried since to get in touch with him," says Hines. "Haven't been able to. But he wrote some great songs." Moore's contributions range from fairly standard love songs like "What Would I Do" and "Explain It to Her Mama" to material demonstrating a note of social consciousness, like "Come On Y'all" and the album's closer, "Our Generation."

It's this last track that is *Electrified*'s main attraction, though Hines terms it "a sleeper, because that was not the song from the album that they had me doing. They had me doing 'Electrified Love' at some shows hosted by [Chicago DJ] Herb Kent." Built on a sweet, loping groove, "Our Generation" has Hines boldly declaring, "Hope of the world is in our generation / It's all left up to us to change this present situation... Our elders taught us one thing but practiced another / Just look what happened to the Indian and the brother." The chorus, meanwhile, sums this all up with a simple, repeated phrase: "Straighten it out." Some twenty years later, this small snippet was looped onto Pete Rock & C.L. Smooth's 1992 single "Straighten It Out."

Today, Hines is pleased with the sample, noting, "The hook sets the groove. Wish it had been my song!" Because Hines didn't write "Our Generation," he was never contacted about the sample. He knew nothing of it until the year 2000, when he walked into the Old School Records in Forest Park, Illinois, and introduced himself to the shop's proprietor, Pete Gianakopoulos, who pointed Hines to the Pete Rock & C.L. Smooth sample.

Through this introduction, Hines learned a bit more about the fate of *Electrified* itself. "Unbeknownst to me, Stax was going down," says Hines. "But Al Bell had turned me over to Jo Bridges and Tom Nixon who had a subsidiary label, We Produce. So that album, after the initial singles, was produced by [them]. It wasn't promoted at all, I found out in later years." The album was supposed to be released on We Produce in 1972, but there is now some question as to whether it was released commercially at all.

Gianakopoulos knew of Hines's work from *The Complete Stax/Volt Soul Singles, Volume 2* box set. "He wrote [Concord Music Group, which owns Stax today] about getting the album released as a reissue," says Hines. "They replied to Pete that they don't know whether that album was ever officially released."

"*Electrified* was never properly pressed and only white label promos came out and never got proper distribution into stores," explains Gianakopoulos. "Probably some cut-out company like Pickwick bought the copies that were pressed, and they hit stores via the cut-out bins."

"Let me hip you on a little something..."

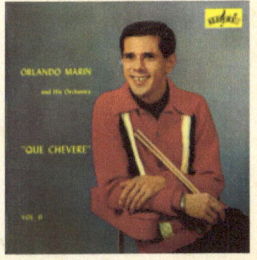
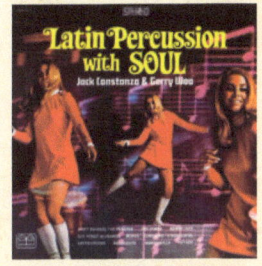
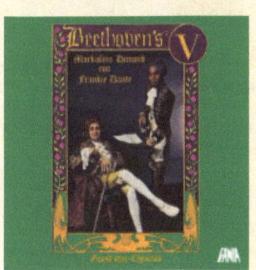

SALSA, SOUL & BOOGALOO
Handpicked by Wax Poetics

150 Gram Vinyl With Promo
Photo & Liner Notes Included

IN STORES SEPTEMBER 2010

ANALOG OUT

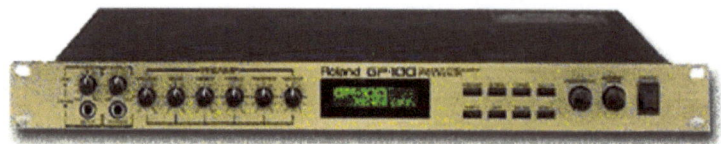

How Guitar Amps and Pedals Became Virtual

Deep in the bowels of any music software lurks a common set of mathematical models for describing sound. Just as with analog circuitry, these are often quite simple at heart, a basic abstraction of how a sound is produced and shaped. It's the way these models are packaged together—the nuanced combination of techniques, interfaces, and the visual skin in which they're wrapped—which transforms math into product. The array of effects and idiosyncratic coloration of amplification employed by guitarists is perhaps the best example of this transition to the virtual, a set of sound design tools that lacks physical form and can even travel on your phone.

The beginning of efforts to model guitar processing digitally had its rough edges. Early attempts at digital distortion simply clipped the digital signal, and since digital clipping doesn't sound like analog clipping, the results could be harsh. (Ironically, that harsh, digital sound is now increasingly sought-after on its own merits, but when first heard, it wasn't exactly a big hit.) These early attempts "contributed to giving digital distortion a 'bad' reputation," says Line 6 founder Marcus Ryle.

Roland was the first on the scene with an emulated model of guitar processing with its 1995 V-Guitar VG-8 and corresponding GP-100 rack unit. The VG-8 described "sound objects" one might find in a guitar signal flow, from vintage amps to pickups and mic placement, via Roland's COSM (Composite Object Sound Modeling) technique. But the Line 6 AxSys 212 deserves the most credit for creating the category to come, claiming the spot as the "world's first digital modeling guitar amplifier." While aimed at guitarists, the AxSys represented a landmark in DSP in general. It's an actual amp, but with virtual effects and amp models built in, all tweakable inside the box, it's an amp that could disguise itself as any other amp and array of effects. Line 6 was granted a U.S. patent (#5,789,689) for modeling vacuum-tube-like distortion, and specifically using oversampling to avoid digital aliasing artifacts, and would later go on to produce popular products like the POD line.

While built into hardware, the models themselves amounted to software—indeed, one might say that the electronics themselves had made sound design a kind of software. That made the transition to computer software a natural one. Line 6's Amp Farm for Pro Tools TDM (1998) established the use of these models as plug-ins, covering the cabinets and amp models. By 2002, IK Multimedia added AmpliTube to the market, which first brought the entire signal chain—stomps, amp, cabinet, mics, and effects—into virtual form, and for native plug-ins (initially Mac RTAS, followed by all other platforms shortly thereafter). Steinberg's Warp VST amp plug-in by Thomas Blug appeared at roughly the same time. Building on their own research into the nature of tubes and vintage gear, industry heavyweights like Native Instruments and, most recently, Waves, have entered their own guitar products.

What's remarkable about the virtual transition is that it makes guitar processing into something as abstract as code, as portable as a musical score, and in hardware as small as a metronome. IK Multimedia recently ported their AmpliTube product to the iPhone, one of a number of rival efforts to make the phone a full guitar signal chain that can fit in your pocket. It's no replacement for an amp, but guitarists are already using these tools as practice tools, since the phone easily outputs to a headphone jack. The trend to virtualization may help repopularize hardware—missing the tangible qualities of interconnected boxes, some musicians are returning to chains of stompboxes and gear. But either way, musicians have access to the compiled wisdom of endless-seeming sonic processors. Whether these grew from the sound of vacuum tubes or were found, as with the wah-wah pedal, in tinkering and mistakes, the sum of sound processing techniques is as accessible as DSP textbooks in a library. ○ Peter Kirn

Thanks to Roger Linn (Roger Linn Design, AdrenaLINN), Tobias Thon (Native Instruments), Starr Ackerman (IK Multimedia), and Marcus Ryle (founder of Line 6) for helping trace the history of virtual guitar processing.

www.ingramcontent.com/pod-product-compliance
Lightning Source LLC
Chambersburg PA
CBHW041702160426
43191CB00003B/55